DOMINIC KIRWAN
Through the Years

Douglas McPherson is a distinguished commentator on the country music scene which he has covered for the past 10 years. Among the publications he has written for are *MOJO*, *Country Music People*, *The Stage*, *What's On in London* and *Classic American*. He is also a regular contributor to *Writers' Forum*.

His love of the country music scene is balanced by the analytical approach of an experienced critic and his understanding of the performers and their background is evident in this book.

This edition first published in 2001
in association with Writers International Ltd
Wessex House,
St Leonards Road,
Bournemouth
BH8 8QS
www.worldwidewriters.com

ISBN: 0-9538101-1-9

Printed by Barnwell's of Aylsham
2-4 Penfold Street,
Aylsham,
Norfolk
NR11 6ET

"I've always admired Dominic. I enjoy his music very much."
- Daniel O'Donnell

Dominic Kirwan is a show business phenomenon, every year playing nearly two hundred packed theatre shows across the UK and Ireland.

Dominic Kirwan - Through the Years traces his career from his childhood as a champion Irish dancer through his singing apprenticeship in the toughest dives of Belfast at the height of the troubles to his current status as an international recording and performing star.

This authorised biography goes behind the scenes of his twelve-year recording career with Ritz Records and his own TV series for Border to reveal the ups, the downs, the mistakes, the successes and the truly FAN-tastic - such as the 40,000 fans who signed a petition to get Dominic on national television.

Through the Years reveals the man behind the music: the loss of his father as a teenager, his reaction to the bomb that hit his home town of Omagh, the night his tour lorry was torched, his intense relationship with his fans and the reality of his relentless tours.

Douglas McPherson's penetrating biography is perhaps the first in-depth study of a British-based country music singing star ■.

"It's not all glamour on the road."
- Philomena Begley

4

DOMINIC KIRWAN
Through the Years

By Douglas McPherson

Starquality Publishing Ltd ● London

Contents

Foreword

By Daniel O'Donnell

I FIRST met Dominic a good few years ago, probably 1986 or 87. We were doing a concert in Omagh. He came to it and we sat and chatted for a good while. I already knew of him. At that time he was not singing as he is now, but he had ambitions to further his career. I remember talking about what I was doing, and I had just started, I suppose, to gain a bit of success about a year or so before. I encouraged him to follow what he was doing, as this is such a wonderful life, and I think he did follow what we call a dream, because that's what music is to people who love doing it. It's not like work, it;s something that you really enjoy, and it's a pleasure to do.

I've always admired Dominic. I enjoy his music very much. I love him singing *Noreen Bawn* because it is a Donegal song, and that's where I come from. So that's definitely a favourite. I also think he is just marvellous with the pop ballads and pop songs. I think that's where his talent really lies.

There's never been any rivalry between us. I would see it, and I am sure Dominic would too, as quite the opposite. I always believe that there's so much room for everybody, and the more that's doing it the better. You can only ever sing in one place at one time.

I had a TV show in 1989 and Dominic guested on that. Since then if ever he would come to a show, I would always ask him to sing. He's very good on stage. He has a good stage presence. But, more than that, he's a nice person, and I think that's more important. To be a performer is one thing, but to be a nice person and to be easy to relate to is more important.

I don't know if Dominic has surpassed what he thought he might achieve, but I think he has accomplished so much and I think there is a lot more for him to do yet. I would always say to him to continue what he is doing. He brings a lot of happiness to a lot of people, and I do wish him lots of success. ■

CHAPTER ONE

Love is in the Air

"ALL I EVER wanted to do was sing," says Dominic Kirwan, "I wanted to be part of a band and be on a show and get on the road. To me that was going to be a success in itself. But then, to get that admiration from your audience, and that respect that they give you in so many, many ways... that has to be something extra, and something special."

"We'll go and see Dominic anywhere," says Martina O'Connell, a fan. "When we go to Ireland and the tapes go in the deck, I'm sure people who see us going along the road singing and waving must think we are crazy. But that's our release. I tell them at work I've had my DK fix. They say, 'Did it do you good?' I say, 'My God, it did.'"

Walking up the hill of Rampant Horse Street, you could feel the excitement in the air. It intensified as you approached the Theatre Royal. It was a beautiful June evening and the sky over Norwich was still bright blue. Many people were out on the pavement, making the most of the balmy weather, or watching out for friends as they arrived by car, taxi and coach. Everyone was looking their best. There was laughter in the air and a cloud of perfume.

Inside the foyer the atmosphere was like a pressure cooker.

Every inch of carpet was covered in freshly-shone female footwear. Bare shoulders in spaghetti strapped dresses jostled with freshly-pressed blouses and sharply-cut sequinned jackets. Heads freshly styled from the salon turned about in the melee, seeking pre-booked tickets and renewing acquaintances. Lips were painted red. Eye-lids sparkled. A blush of excitement shone through smoothly powdered cheeks.

There weren't many men present, but they were there. "We go to see Dominic all over England, Ireland, Scotland and Wales," says a 27-year-old male nurse, Chris Sills, who was first hooked on Dominic at the age of 17. "Everyone says how can you go to all these shows. But they're all different."

"How many shows do we go to?" asks Elizabeth Ashfield.

"In a year, maybe 50" says husband Paul. "Obviously I'm in a minority, but I don't just get dragged along kicking and screaming. I enjoy the shows very much. It's a good night out."

The reason for the rare build up of excitement smiled benignly from a poster behind the merchandise stand where money, CDs, scarves and programmes were changing hands with the gusto of a bull market on the London Stock Exchange. As well as the posters, the face gazed out from the covers of three concert videos and eleven CDs and cassettes stretching back over ten years of recording. The face also gazed, in a variety of different shots, from t-shirts, key rings, coasters, badges, mouse mats, sun visors, mugs, fridge magnets. The demand for the Kirwan image was insatiable.

"At the end of the show they *run* at you," says Dominic, still registering disbelief at the demand for merchandise.

Peter McGlone, Dominic's personal assistant and the brains behind much of the merchandise; from pens to golf umbrellas adorned with a giant DK, tells a story about a woman who bought a Dominic Kirwan calendar only to find the spiral that held the pages together was broken. Having sold out, Peter was unable to exchange the item, but the fan refused his offer of her money back, preferring to have a broken calendar rather than none at all.

The changing faces on the CD covers told the story of a man who had grown up in the music business. The cover of the earliest album, *Try A Little Kindness*, showed a heavy-set lad in a none-too-flattering dark shirt. His barber shop short back and sides erupted in an atomic mushroom of unruly curls above his ears. He was standing awkwardly with his hands on his hips, his eyes narrowed above a grin, as if unused to the glare of the limelight.

The face on the latest posters and CD cover was more suave and assured. It was a handsome, open, guileless face with neatly groomed wavy hair, an easy smile and pale blue eyes that seemed to melt the heart and stir the loins of every woman who gazed upon them. The face was unlined, far too young for a man three days short of his fortieth birthday.

The packed house was not an isolated occurrence. According to the manager of another Norfolk theatre, The Princess in Hunstanton, "The day after our season's programme comes out and it says we've got Dominic Kirwan on, they're queuing up at the box office door from five o'clock in the morning. On the evening they're lined up around the block."

Fan Gill Marseilles offers a reason: "I have seen Tom Jones, Sinatra, Neil Diamond, Pavarotti and Domingo and I think he knocks them all into a cocked hat".

Attesting to Dominic's appeal across barriers of age and sex is sprightly 71-year-old John Smith. "I sit there clapping away and singing and all these ladies are looking at me thinking, 'What's he on!' But we enjoy it, the wife and I. We travel for miles."

In the dressing room behind the stage Alison Conner had a job that would have made her the envy of many of the women busily finding their seats just a few feet away. Charged for the past ten years with the job of keeping Dominic and his band looking like stars, Ali, as she is known to all backstage, was at that moment holding Dominic's freshly ironed stage trousers while the singer peeled off his jeans to reveal powerful legs and white Calvin Klein boxer shorts.

Ali's selfless dedication was typical of the devotion Dominic inspired in those around him. For the past decade she had packed her ironing board in the back of her car and driven herself to and from every theatre that Dominic played on the mainland, despite holding down a job as a teacher.

"My current car is two years old and has about sixty thousand miles on the clock, " says Ali, who took on her mother-like role because she didn't want to let the singer loose with an iron on the first stage clothes she made him. Describing Dominic as more of a friend than a boss, Ali recalls her endless motorway travels. "When you set off for Inverness with a nine-hour journey in front of you it seems a long way, but it's surprising how quickly it goes. "

In the flesh, Dominic looked much more rugged than on the posters. He was just as handsome but looked much more of a man's man. His face was deeply tanned. He wasn't as tall as he looked on stage; nobody is. But although he wasn't particularly big, there was a hint of brawn about the former champion traditional Irish dancer who had once made a living selling car parts in Northern Ireland. There was a leathery toughness about him and, when he spoke, his deep voice had a gruff masculinity that could surprise anybody who had only seen his stage persona. A lady-killer he might be, but there was nothing effete about the boy from Omagh.

Most of all, there was an undeniable star quality even in his current trouserless state. Somehow, in person far more than in photographs, which didn't always do him justice, he always carried himself with a hint of James Dean in those immortal movie posters of the 1950s; cool but brooding, never lightweight.

At that moment, Dominic was psyching himself up for his

performance. A portable CD/cassette player on a chair in the corner was helping him. Half an hour earlier it had been playing a tape he used for his vocal exercises. Now it was cranking out urgent, pumping R'n'B. Not overly loud. Just enough to set the room jumping.

One of Dominic's early and enduring heroes, Elvis Presley, used to get in the mood for his Vegas concerts by playing the Jerry Lee Lewis album *The Greatest Live Show On Earth*. Dominic favoured much more obscure American acts on tapes supplied by a friend. He was listening not just to the adrenalin-raising music, but also for any patter that he might be able to use in his show.

"You never know what you might pick up," he reasons, "and you know nobody over here has ever heard it."

Pulling on his black stage suit, Dominic turned to the mirror, dusting his face with make up for the lights and smoothing his immaculate hair. Normally relaxed and easy, his movements now were quick and almost hyper as the clock ticked towards show time.

It had been a long tour. Sixty dates since February, most of them one-nighters. He'd kicked off at the glamorous sounding Carnegie Hall, in the not-so-glamorous Dunfermline. Since then he'd criss-crossed the country playing mostly consecutive nights on a schedule seemingly designed to eat up as many motorway miles as possible. Up to Burnley, down to Dorking, across to Chesterfield, then to Blackpool, across to York. The gigs themselves varied. It was mostly theatres and concert halls. But he'd also fitted in a dance at the Galtymore Irish club in London's Cricklewood and two nights of cabaret at the intimate Stardust Club in Leicester alongside dates that more accurately reflected his popularity: three nights at the Grand Opera House in Belfast, three nights in Ayr and two-night stands in Inverness, Arbroath, Hunstanton and Swindon.

As ever, Dominic's duties to his fans took up many more hours than just the ones he spent on stage.

"He's a really genuine, kind man who always has time to chat, sign and pose for photographs," reports Margaret Cavany from Yorkshire. "We went to Ireland to see Dominic and he stopped rehearsals to chat to us and have photos taken with us."

"I don't think he feels like we mob him," gushed mini-skirted sisters Diane and Jane, who, "Go to as many shows as we can," and always wait behind to speak to their hero. "If he didn't have time he'd tell us. But he's just so sociable. He's got time for everybody, young or old. He's a lovely, lovely, genuine man."

The final day on the tour had been a hectic and emotional one, including hooking up for lunch with his sisters Catherine and Theresa, and their children, who lived on the mainland and would be unable to join him in Ireland for his birthday.

Dominic was tired. And he knew he wouldn't get much sleep after the show. He'd have to grab what he could in the car as Peter drove him through the night to catch the boat home at 5am. He was looking forward to a few days' welcome break, to spending some precious time at home with his family, and then to flying out to Nashville to record what was being talked about as the most important album of his career.

At that moment, though, Dominic pushed his tiredness aside, determined to be at his best for the paying public, many of whom had travelled great distances to see him.

Some of the fans had been with him for ten years now, since he first signed to Ritz Records and made his first tours of the mainland as support act to American country legends Kenny Rogers, Charley Pride and Tammy Wynette. Some had been with him twice that long, since the days when, as little more than a boy, he had struggled to juggle the responsibility of a full-time job and the demands of a new marriage and fatherhood with the dream of playing weekend gigs around his home town in County Tyrone.

"I still get people come up to me and say, 'You sang at our wedding. Tonight we're celebrating our 20th anniversary.'"

For Dominic, those twenty years had often been hard. But there was not a single evening in that time when he had not found his greatest rewards in walking through the wings into the spotlights and the rush of screams and applause that came to meet him like an express train. And still, after two decades, he remained hungry for more. He was hungry to take his career further.

His main aim would have been to get a Number One says Dominic's younger sister, Catherine DeLacy. "To this day I'd say that's still his main aim."

Dominic was not a boastful man, but neither did he suffer from the insecurity of some performers or the complacency of others. He knew he was good and he knew he had yet to realise his full potential. Yes, he could and did fill theatres this size the length and breadth of the county. Ignored by a mainstream media that almost daily made instant -though often fleeting- stars of performers with far less natural talent, he had clawed his way up to this level, almost by word of mouth, always giving his all in the knowledge that every new fan who saw him would come back again and spread the word to others. Dominic loved those fans as much as they loved him. But he also knew that there were many, many more people in the wider market who had yet to hear of him.

To reach them, Dominic needed the exposure of a hit record.

Fellow Irishman and Ritz artist Daniel O'Donnell, who some saw as Dominic's closest rival, had already made that leap. Daniel had made several visits to the pop charts. He had appeared on Top Of The Pops. He guested on TV chat shows like Mrs Merton and got national press coverage for his famous tea parties which saw hundreds of fans make an annual pilgrimage to his home in Donegal. The phenomenon of those tea parties had even inspired a hit West End play, *Women On The Verge Of HRT*, that focused on the lives and aspirations of two of his middle-aged fans.

It was true that people made jokes about Daniel. One of the favourites was, 'What has a hundred legs and no teeth? The front row at a Daniel O'Donnell concert.' But it was Daniel who had the last laugh, because the jokes only meant he had achieved the household name status of his equally clean-living hero, Cliff Richard.

Dominic knew he was capable of making the same commercial leap, if not a bigger one. He was confident that he had the talent, style and credibility to appeal to the youth audience that went wild for bands like Westlife and Boyzone. He also had a voice that could compete with Tom Jones for the more mature market. But he also knew, particularly tonight, as he approached the last gig before his 40th birthday, that he didn't have forever left to do it.

He looked at his watch. Not long to go.

Normally Dominic performed two high-energy sets, eschewing the convention of an opening act in the belief that audiences buy tickets to see the headliner and that they deserve maximum value for their money. On this tour, however, he had decided to let his band open with a half-hour set of their own. Artistically, it was not one of his better decisions.

Pianist and Musical Director Jim McVeigh was a good singer who also backed Dominic with harmony vocals on stage. He had only been with the band for a couple of years but already he looked as if he'd been there for ever. He and Dominic made a great comic double act, with McVeigh a perfect straight man. Dominic would pretend to be angry with the rotund pianist over some misdemeanour and the glum-faced McVeigh would milk the audience for maximum sympathy, walking off stage with his head hanging low when Dominic refused to introduce him alongside the rest of the band. Then Jim would get the final, biggest laugh with some doleful rejoinder.

Although he harboured no ambitions to be a star, McVeigh was capable of entertaining the house with a few songs. The rest of the band offered less value as front men. The drummer, in particular, should never have taken his turn to sing and, fully exploiting the relaxed end of tour atmosphere, guitarist Seamus Rooney resorted to changing into a woman's dress to get a laugh when he sang the Dolly Parton song *Old Flames*. The fans of any other artist might have started booing and walking out at that stage. A review in *Country Music People* asked, "Why was Kirwan inflicting such dross on his fans?"

But the love that Dominic's audience felt for their hero extended to those around him. Like Dominic, they were more than happy to indulge his hard working and efficient band in a bit of harmless fun.

Then, when the larkiness was over, it was time for the main attraction.

Dominic grabbed his cordless microphone from the dressing room table. He stood alone for a moment with his back to the black curtain at the side of the stage. His back ramrod straight he took some deep breaths. He recited to himself the simple prayer he always said before going on stage. Then he heard Jim make the introduction: "Please give a warm welcome to Mr Dominic... Kir-wan!"

For a moment the screams and applause threatened to drown the band. Then, as Dominic bounded on to the stage, the noise actually did drown out all else. As if in mime, the steel guitarist was slapping his hands together above his head and the entire house took his lead in clapping along, with a force that seemed to shake the building.

On the edge of his consciousness, Dominic saw the smiles on the faces of Jim and his backing vocalist Trionagh Moore as they turned to watch his entrance. He smiled back, but already he was lost in the lights and applause.

He hit centre stage with perfect timing to go straight into his opening number, the highly appropriate *Love Is In The Air*. Moving with the up tempo rhythm, he used the entire surface of the stage, repeatedly going right to the edge where he could see past the spotlights and make eye contact with the fans. An Australian admirer had recently set up an Internet website on which she had christened him No Greater Gyrator and he lived up to the tag, swivelling his hips and pulling mock-smouldering expressions that drew squeals from the crowd.

The song ended and without pausing for breath, Dominic changed moods, going into the romantic ballad *I Swear*. The song was a killer. It had already been a huge American country hit for John Michael Montgomery and an international pop hit for the group N'Sync. But neither of those artists invested it with the emotional resonance and sheer vocal power that Dominic projected.

As he hit the climatic note, Dominic felt exhilarated. His voice sounded good and the band, simultaneously loosened up and tightened up by the many, many dates behind them, were playing like a dream.

"I think it's going to be one of those nights!" he told the audience and it was clear they were up for it, too. The song *The Answer To Everything* called for him to sing the line, "Do you love me?" And the roar of "Yeees!" that came back was deafening. The fans were also in good voice when Dominic turned the microphone towards them and invited them to sing the chorus of the old Bellamy Brothers hit *If I Said You Had A Beautiful Body Would You Hold It Against Me?*

"You'll have to give me time to think about that one!" he teased them, grinning.

By the end of the second song the first present had arrived on the edge of the stage: a brightly wrapped champagne bottle with a silvery balloon bearing the number 40 floating high above it on a length of string. Other offerings arrived as the show went on: single red roses, gift-wrapped boxes of chocolates, bouquets of flowers, teddy bears and more bottles, many of which also had 40th Birthday balloons tied to them.

Dominic moved some of the gifts towards the sides of the stage so that nobody's view would be spoiled. Then he smiled as he went into the song that would really bring out the present giving instinct. As he began to sing A *Sprig Of Irish Heather* there was a mass upheaval in the auditorium as hundreds of handbags were opened as one. In a ritual that had been enacted countless times in theatres and concert halls throughout the country, bottom after bottom left their seats and the aisles creaked under the weight of women hurrying towards the front of the stage with sprigs of heather held out before them.

Dominic went down on to the carpet in front of the stage to meet the onslaught and was immediately seized upon. A queue formed on each side of him. Barely able to breathe or utter a word, he turned rapidly from one queue to the other, surrendering himself to a hug and a kiss from virtually every woman in the building. Thin, fat, young and old, the lines showed no signs of coming to an end as Jim began to lead the band back into the song for a second time. Some of the women tried to tell him something and he tried his best in the seconds available to respond sincerely. Everyone gave him a sprig of heather, which he began handing in bunches to a helper who passed them onto the stage. Some brought yet more colourful wrapped presents. Others draped tinsel around his shoulders and over his head and sprinkled him with glitter dust.

"You're better than Daniel!" yelled one admirer, snaking an arm around his neck and pulling his ear towards her mouth.

"Sorry?" said Dominic, deftly swinging his microphone towards her.

"You're better than Daniel!" she repeated and this time the entire theatre heard her. Many called out their agreement and Dominic feigned embarrassment, milking the moment for laughter.

When the last of the women had snatched her moment of satisfaction, Dominic hurried back up the steps to the stage. His nostrils full of perfume and the taste of lipstick on his lips, he heard an unexpected roar of laughter behind him and turned to see a little bald man, lips puckered, where the queue of femininity had been.

Dominic mimed a barely exaggerated mixture of horror and disbelief to win more laughter from the crowd. Then, to howls, he got on his knees, leaned over the edge of the stage and planted a kiss on the old man's head.

He'd been right, thought Dominic as the band charged into the next song, it was going to be one of those nights.

In fact, Dominic recognised the bald man, although it was no set-up.

"It first happened a couple of years ago, and it was just a spontaneous thing," Dominic recalls, "We were having a bit of fun with the heather thing and obviously it's usually the ladies who come up. Out of the blue this guy came up. He was at a level where I was looking down at him. I saw this bald head and I thought, well, OK, I'm not going to kiss you on the lips but what the hell. He loved it and the audience loved it. It got a good laugh. So now whenever we're in that region he comes with his piece of heather. He obviously enjoys it as much as everybody else."

After an hour and a half at the top of his game, Dominic began to feel the exertion catching up with him. His jacket, tie and waistcoat gone, his white shirt was soaked with sweat. As he began to rattle through the many dedications, and there were seemingly hundreds of them -Marge from Norwich, Jenny and Dave from Cambridge, Dorothy who's celebrating her 89th birthday- he fought to recover his breath and swallow the overwhelming emotions he felt rising up within him, stirred by the love that he had been bathed in night after night for the last four months.

His hair clinging in ringlets to his gleaming brow, he thanked the audience for coming. Normally he stayed behind after every show to sign autographs and talk to anyone who wanted to meet him. Sometimes the queue of fans kept him at a theatre until 3.30 in the morning. And he happily indulged them, even when he was ill. Tonight, however, he told them that the journey ahead of him would make staying behind impossible. He spoke with genuine regret and, of course, they understood as he knew they would. As the applause filled the theatre, he let his head drop forward, deeply humbled.

He was exhausted. He knew he had already put more effort into his show than most performers. He knew not a soul in the house would be disappointed if he went home now and he knew it might be better for his health and his voice if he did so. But, like an athlete smashing through the pain barrier, he dredged deep inside himself for the reserves to carry on.

Revelling in his diversity, he sang the Englebert Humperdinck hit *Please Release Me* as the hard hitting, emotionally anguished country song it was written as, the big, powerful notes seeming to impale themselves like thrown knives and axes into the walls at the back of the theatre. He created a party atmosphere as he danced through the Latin pop of *Ten Guitars* and he turned up the heat with the thumping rock'n'roll of *I Love A Rainy Night,* effortlessly stoking the lust of his female admirers with his playfully lascivious delivery of the line, "It makes me ffffeel good!"

Time and again he delivered ballads of finale-like proportions and time and again he managed to find more to give.

The climax was *The Town I Love So Well*. Written by Phil Coulter, it was an old song about the Irish troubles that had first been recorded by The Dubliners in the early 1970s. Dominic had known the words most of his life. But since the IRA bomb that had ripped apart his home town two years before he had sung the song as if it had been written especially for him.

At nearly ten minutes long the song was an epic, telling the story of a man who leaves a poor but contented childhood in

Ireland and becomes successful across the water only to return home and be confronted by a town 'brought to its knees by the armoured cars and the bombed-out bars". The parallels with Dominic's own life were impossible to miss, down to the detail about "earning his first pay in a small pick-up band", and his reading gripped the attention like a vice, burning deep into the dramatic lyric and making it sound like an autobiography. When he reached the anguished line, "The damned barbed wire gets higher and higher..." he thought as always about Omagh and the bomb that had prompted him to bring the song back into his repertoire.

Dominic had always thought of the bustling market town as a shining example of how the religious communities of Northern Ireland could live in harmony, so he felt more than most people a deep sense of anger that the place would now be forever associated with the much publicised atrocity that had torn its heart out.

Dominic had no intention of becoming a politician, but he had raised, through appeals at his concerts, more than £30,000 for the victims of the bomb. He knew the money was inadequate. Any amount of money would be. Because in a town the size of Omagh Dominic, as one of its most prominent and much loved citizens, had known many, if not most, of the people or at least the families of the people, who had died or been injured in the blast. He had spoken to many who had not worked since. He knew families who would feel the effect of the bombing for generations.

The first time he had sung *The Town I Love So Well* after the atrocity had been in Scotland on the day the first burials had taken place. Dominic had broken down, unable to finish the song. Many in the audience had also been overcome, with TV news footage of the funerals only too fresh in their minds.

Two years on, in Norwich, Dominic sang the song with thoughts of the victims in his mind.

He also sang the song with artistic pride. Dominic had yet to release *The Town I Love So Well* on an album, partly because he believed it belonged on an Irish-themed record whereas his recent releases had been more geared towards the mainstream, and partly because he knew the lyric could be misinterpreted and open to political controversy. It had been banned by some radio stations when The Dubliners released it.

There were others, however, who believed that *The Town I Love So Well* could be the career hit that Dominic was searching for, not least because of the way it tapped so powerfully into the Zeitgeist of the Northern Irish peace process. True, its length would be an obstacle to easy acceptance into a radio playlist. But sometimes it was the songs that refused to fit into any established mould that became the greatest successes. And sometimes, as in the case of Don McLean's *American Pie*, that included very long songs.

Whether it could be single material or otherwise, the song was by far the strongest that Dominic had ever tackled. There was a hard edge to the song and a weight to the material that raised his credibility as an artist far above that of the easy listening country 'n'' Irish crooner that most people who knew him only by name believed him to be.

As he reached the song's climax, with its deeply human plea for a brighter day at the end of the darkness, he felt triumphant and empowered; invincible, as only a true contender for greatness can ever feel.

The audience felt the full force of both Dominic's pride and the humanitarian message of the song. As one they rose to their feet, clapping until their palms were sore.

For a second, Dominic savoured the moment. Then, seizing the tidal wave of adoration he turned the mood on its head, leading the band into an exuberant cover of The Mavericks' recent big hit *Dance The Night Away.*

Like a dam-burst of emotion the already standing audience

flooded forward towards the edge of the stage. In the balcony they began to leave their seats by the hundreds, feet pounding on the woodwork as they swarmed downstairs to add to the crush.

Dominic could hardly get to the edge of the stage for presents that continued to be placed there. But he stepped over them, reaching forward to clasp the many hands that reached towards him. Each one he shook gripped him with a fleeting, desperate passion, not wanting to let go. As the music swam around him and the mass of faces and bodies pressed forward, he saw lips mouthing the words, "I love you."

Energised and invigorated, Dominic clung to the moment like a lover who doesn't want to leave his woman. His final, climatic thrust was *The Wonder Of You*, a great, powerful love song made famous by his early and enduring hero, Elvis Presley. The song was associated with The King's latter years, but Dominic looked, sounded and felt like a man at his absolute peak.

Eventually, as it had to, the curtain came down. The musicians left their instruments. But the music didn't stop. Filling the auditorium with pride and love, everyone in the house sang Happy Birthday to the greatest entertainer any one of them had ever seen. ■

CHAPTER TWO

Buy me a Rose

ANOTHER day, another dressing room. Two hours before his show, Dominic is sitting in a swivel chair with his back to a row of wall mirrors. He's wearing dark blue narrow leg jeans, a black shirt and shiny black leather slip-ons. His thigh- length black leather jacket is most definitely staying on. Dominic has a chest infection that refuses to budge. The lilac painted dressing room is as cold as a morgue and nobody can get any heat out of the single radiator.

Later, on stage, Dominic will crack a joke about it. "Is it hot out there?" He asks the crowd, rubbing his hands together. "I was freezing earlier. Luckily a lady came to my dressing room and warmed me up." He lets a collective "Ooooh" rise to the suggestiveness of the remark, before getting a laugh with the innocent elaboration: "With two electric heaters!"

Most things that happen to Dominic during the day find their way into his act. Such as Jim McVeigh being interviewed by *Keyboard Player* magazine that afternoon. "They didn't want to talk to *me*," Dominic will pretend to moan in the latest episode of on stage banter with his pianist.

"I don't know how it all started," says the tubby McVeigh, who is far jollier off stage than is suggested by his doleful, straight man role in the exchanges with his boss. "We don't rehearse those things. The other day, for example, we had to miss a show because Dominic went up to Leeds to do a television spot and he got stuck in a horrendous traffic jam on the way back. So at the next show I said, 'You haven't told them what happened to you last night.' So he told the audience the story. Then I said, 'and what was the first thing you had to do when you got out of that traffic jam?' So, of course, he had to say, 'I had to go to the toilet!'"

But that's later. Right now, folding his arms and hunching into his jacket against the cold while Ali puts the kettle on, Dominic is being quizzed about the heather giving ritual that is a staple of his concerts. It's not a unique aspect of his concert career. A few years earlier, he used to perform a song called *A Daisy A Day* which saw his female fans lining up at the stage to exchange bunches of daisies for kisses. That particular tradition reached a hilarious zenith at a gig in Telford when two of his most ardent fans cantered up to the stage in the costume of a pantomime cow with a sign saying 'Hello, I'm Daisy,' hanging from the animal's neck.

Despite his cheerful acceptance of that particular stunt, Dominic has mixed views on audience participation, realising that one person's moment of sharing the spotlight with a star might be just a distraction or a spoilt view for somebody else who wants to sit back and enjoy the show. He has just recorded a stunning ballad called *Buy Me A Rose*, which was a big hit on the American country charts for Kenny Rogers. Announcing the imminent release of the song, one country magazine jokily warned florists to get in extra stock in anticipation of Dominic's hordes of smitten fans taking the title literally. In fact, since bringing the number into his concerts, Dominic has taken the bold and unusual step of firmly telling the audience not to give him roses during the song. Although he knows his decision might offend some of his fans, he argues, "It's just too good a song to break into it like that whereas *A Sprig Of Irish Heather*, although it's an old Irish song, it's more of a throwaway type of song."

A few nights previously, a single brave fan dared to test his no roses policy only to be stopped in her tracks with an upturned palm and a 'don't even think about it' look that a traffic policeman would have been proud of.

Dominic accepts, however, that the heather ritual is "just a bit of fun."

Dismissing the potential dangers of submitting himself to a public mauling, the gruff voiced singer says, "The only way it could get out of control is if it's a very long queue and I haven't got through the queue and I'm moving on to the next song. Then I've thought, 'well, the next song I can still handle myself through this but I need to get finished by the end of *that*. . .' and if I'm running out of time and I think I'm not going to be back on stage. . . that's where the problems can occur. Then you get situations in certain theatres where people can't get to you from the centre so they come from the sides and you're trying to work both sides of the building. It's the time factor. It's not the fact that people are coming to you and giving you your gift."

As for over-amorous fans. . . Dominic looks away from his interviewer and shares a conspiratorial look with Peter McGlone, his personal assistant and constant companion of the past decade, although the two go back much further than that.

A dapper man in his fifties, McGlone has just driven Dominic to the venue from his hotel in his maroon Mitsubishi Shogun with the M1 DOM number plate. Much loved by Dominic's fans, McGlone is a gentle, quietly spoken, pink-faced man and something of a father figure to Dominic, who lost his father when he was 17. There always seems to be a twinkle in Peter's eyes and a smile is never far from his lips. He's smiling now, and his eyes are definitely twinkling as they lock with Dominic's, the two men silently enjoying the empathy that comes from spending many, many years on the road together.

For a moment Dominic seems to be seeking guidance in the older man's eyes. Perhaps he's pondering how much to reveal. Perhaps he's wondering which side of his character is best suited to fielding this particular line of enquiry – the demure and sincere gentleman who visits the sick in his local hospital every Christmas morning, or the cocky working class lad with a ready wink who looks like he's just walked off a building site. But McGlone isn't helping him on this one. Realising he's on his own, Dominic tries to contain a smile as he says, with some, but not too much, embarrassment in his gravelly voice, "You might get the odd *grab*, or the odd *nip*. . ." The smile refuses to be contained, and a grin is right behind it. "What else can you say?" He splutters, crossing his ankles, and trying to look serious again. "It's all a bit of fun."

His serious face taking hold, the singer continues, "You go to some shows where the act does a bit of mingling and you see the heavies with him. . ." Dominic wrinkles his nose in disapproval. "I suppose at times you need somebody beside you to take things off you. But you don't need heavies. Your audience are not there to cause you problems, they're there to support you. They want to get that little peck on the cheek, or that shake of the hand for that matter, but that's all they're there for. They're not there to harm you."

How does it feel to be the centre of so much female attention? With a knowing smile, Dominic considers the question. He's clearly mindful that having a large female following can distract a media that's all to willing to be distracted, from more important matters such as the music. A prime example is the constant references to the knicker-throwing fans of Tom Jones. Another is Daniel O'Donnell's gran's army. In his own case, Dominic knows that his current interviewer, while fulsome in his praise of the singer, has also devoted a fair few column inches to satirising his heart-throb status. A review of Dominic's 1998 compilation album, *The*

Collection, began. *For his predominantly older, female fans, a Dominic Kirwan concert is like mass instant hormone replacement treatment. Like Viagra he should be available on the NHS.*

Perhaps remembering those words, Dominic's response is beautifully weighted.

"I think you've got to appreciate it and understand it the best you can. I know many people can be flippant and tongue in cheek about it, and laugh at it. . ." No names no pack drill, but he knows, and his interviewer knows, exactly who he's talking about. . . "But the way I look at it is if they were in the same position they would accept it. So when I read a review and the critic is having that little jibe at it, I just smile to myself and think, 'you wish you were there,' or whatever, you know?"

His interviewer concedes, with a smile, that he's been nailed, and Dominic, knowing he's nailed him, concludes mildly, "so it doesn't bother me. I appreciate it."

More problematic, all be it an enviable problem to have, is the sheer quantity of gifts that Dominic receives from his followers.

"It started very early in my career. You met the fans, you spoke to them and they got to know a bit more about you. In my case, I was a young father with a young family. They knew I was out working and grafting at what I was doing and trying to make a better life. People wanted to give something because they thought they were getting so much of you and your time, with the music. So it started at a very early time and it's something that has built up over the years".

"In some cases it's maybe not as plentiful as it used to be. I don't mind that. I don't go on stage looking for presents."

Today, Ali takes responsibility for distributing the flowers and cuddly toys to hospitals and hospices close to the venues. The bottles are shared with the band and served up at parties. "Unless it's a really good bottle of red, or something. . ."

"Or champagne," puts in McGlone.

". . .Then I'll say, 'I'll have that.'"

That still leaves Dominic with a stock of fine wines and whiskies that he will never live long enough to drink. And much else besides, all of it crammed into the loft of his modern, detached mock-Tudor house in Bracken Close, Omagh.

"I moved from a three-bedroom house to a four-bedroom house and one of the thoughts in the back of my head was, 'I'm gonna have an attic that's floored.' That's all I was thinking about; 'I'm gonna have an attic that's floored.' We got it floored and I was thinking, 'God, look at the amount of room up here.' It was unbelievable. I thought, 'We'll never fill this.' Now you can't get in the attic."

Dominic is quick to point out that he is in no way ungrateful for the gifts that fill his roof space, although as he prepares to move once again to a house he is having built on the outskirts of Omagh, the hoard is very much on his mind. One of the versatile Ali's next assignments is to venture into the Kirwan attic and attempt to catalogue what is up there.

The constant deluge also puts Dominic's family in a quandary when it comes to Christmas and his birthday.

"I've received so many flowers and gifts over the years and had people sending flowers to my home that it's given my family serious difficulties in buying me presents. Because I get many really good presents as well. This leather jacket I'm wearing was a present. So, if your wife wants to buy you a leather jacket you already have one."

Dominic pushes up the cuff of the said garment.

"Not this particular watch, but I've been given watches, shirts, clothes. . . things that your family would think of choosing for you. So I suppose in one respect it's great to get it all, and to accept it and appreciate it, but in another way it's very difficult for your family because you really close the doors on them.

"It's become very simple at home. On the likes of a Valentine they would not get flowers. They'd get a card and that's it. Because flowers. . . they're not meaningless, but they're so plentiful that they become not what they should be."

Not that all the presents Dominic receives are in the leather jacket class. Later, as a freshly-changed Dominic prepares to go on stage, Ali brings into the dressing room some of the cards, letters and packages that have been handed in for Dominic on the merchandise stand in the foyer. During his first set she'll sort them out into requests, dedications and letters to be answered. The dedications she'll copy on to fresh sheets of paper to save Dominic stumbling over impenetrable handwriting when he reads them out in the second half of the show.

The room is buzzing to the sound of Hargus & Moe rapping out *I've Got My Mojo Working* on the cassette player.

Resplendent in his pink stage suit, with just a minute or two till show time, Dominic plucks an interesting looking small brown jiffy bag from the pile and rips it open.

He reads aloud, "With all the people you meet on your travels I thought this might come in handy."

From the package he pulls a small, cheap blue address book. He raises an eyebrow in a way that Roger Moore would have been proud of. Just what he really needed. . .

"I buy him everything with ducks on," says white-haired Connie Verley, who is known to Dominic as The Duchess.

Ducks?

"Duck walking sticks, duck toast racks. . ."

Ye-es, but why ducks?

Laughing, the Duchess confesses she's not really sure. "It started when I gave him a box of fudge and it had a big duck attached to it. He said later, 'Thanks for the duck, Connie,' and since then it's gone on from there. Louise, his wife, has got them at home, displayed in lots of places."

Dominic's show is long over. Leisure centre staff are moving noisily between the rows of empty seats, picking up litter and sending loud metallic echoes through the cavernous gymnasium-cum-auditorium. But Connie and her friends

Fran and Martina have stayed behind, in the raised seats towards the back, to talk about an obsession that has governed their lives for the past dozen years. The three of them are the core of a gang sometimes numbering as many as 17, that travel all over England and Ireland, seeing as many Dominic Kirwan shows as they possibly can.

"My husband says he reckons he's bought Dominic his Rolex watch!" says Martina, who likes to see Dominic at least once a month and thinks nothing of interrupting a holiday following Dominic around Ireland to fly back to the mainland to see yet another of his shows.

The fact that many of Dominic's most ardent followers have husbands and respectable jobs only makes their infatuation with the singer more remarkable. Martina insists the attraction, in her case at least, is not sexual and that she doesn't flirt with the singer.

"We have a laugh with him and maybe the odd joke that could be twisted, but there is nothing there like that. No. Definitely not."

You don't find him attractive?

The three women throw their heads back with laughter. "Well yeah, but not in that way. I mean, he's been called everything. . ."

"Sex on legs," puts in Fran.

"But no, we don't look on him like that. We've got husbands. We've got lives. And he's a family man. He's a very proud family man."

Attempting to explain her reason for following Dominic so obsessively, Martina continues: "It's not like we're middle aged groupies. It really is a fantastic night out. We don't drink, we don't smoke. . . My son often says, 'Mum, you're a sad case.' And I say, 'I don't have to get drunk to enjoy myself.'" She holds up a bottle of mineral water to make her point. "That and a concert ticket is all it takes."

In fact, Martina is quick to stress that she and her friends are not the most obsessed of Dominic fans. Apart from Connie and her ducks, they distance themselves from the present givers and the heather bearers. Except, of course, on special occasions such as Dominic's birthday.

"There are people who will do six or seven nights in a row. Personally I couldn't do that. Two nights, yes. Three nights in a row when we're in Ireland. . . we couldn't handle more than three nights in a row. We have to work. We've got lives.

"There are some really adoring fans who know everything about him. There are probably one or two who are quite obsessed and he's their life. But if that gives them happiness, without hurting anybody, that's fine."

Analyse the comments of Dominic's most regular concert-goers and the predominant phrases are not the obvious ones like "He's a great singer," or "He's a fabulous entertainer." The word that comes up time and time again is Dominic's "Sincerity." Not just the sincerity with which a singer interprets a lyric, but the sincerity Dominic displays in his extended meetings with fans after every show.

Country singers, generally, are expected to be more approachable than their pop counterparts where the retinue of bodyguards and dark glasses adds to the untouchable appeal of a Madonna or Michael Jackson. Country singers, traditionally, are expected to be one of the people even when, in the case of those American country singers who have acquired great wealth and hugely extravagant lifestyles, they are clearly not. Dominic, however, takes his relationship with his fans to extremes, particularly impressing them with his memory for faces and names.

"It's the way he always appreciates his fans and makes time for them," says Brenda Morrissey, who has seen nearly 600 Dominic concerts. "He invariably comes out to chat to everyone. It isn't just a quick hello, next please, which is how it seems with Daniel, but the genuine concern he has for people. He knows the majority of his fans by name, even though these now number thousands. He must have a superb memory, because you can mention something to him, and he may bring it up in conversation several months later."

"It's amazing how many fans he does recognise and knows by name. Even people that don't go that often." says Paul Ashfield.

"He's lovely to talk to off stage," says Paul's wife, Elizabeth. "If anybody's got any problems, he's always ready to listen."

Perhaps because so many fans make themselves so known to him, Dominic notices when they are not at their local gigs. Peter McGlone relates how, driving through the night after a show, Dominic will often say, "I didn't see so and so there tonight."

Fan John Smith makes the same point. "At Hunstanton we got there early and we were loitering around the theatre when Dominic arrived. I went and said, 'How do you do,' and he said, 'Where's your wife?' He was that interested."

Martina O'Connell adds, "If he hasn't seen somebody for a long time, he'll ask after them."

The depth of Dominic's feelings for his fans is best expressed by his reaction to them in times of crisis. Connie Verley has received cheering phone calls from Dominic when she was going through a difficult patch.

Brenda Morrissey relates the following story of Dominic's response to one fan's death: "We were at one of his concerts in Bridlington one Saturday evening a few years back when Dominic learnt that one of his fans from Peterborough had died of leukaemia a couple of days previously. When we saw him in the queue after the show, he asked if we could find out when the funeral was, as he would like to attend if possible. I made some enquiries when I arrived home the following day, Sunday, to discover that the funeral was the next morning. Dominic had given me a number where he could be contacted on Sunday evening, so I rang him and let him know the details. Dominic was recording his album *On The Way To A Dream* at Bromsgrove on the Monday. However, he popped into the studio early Monday morning to let them know his plans. Then he and Peter drove down to Peterborough -about a hundred miles- attended the funeral, spoke to the chief mourners, and then drove back to Bromsgrove where Dominic continued his recording. I can't think of any other performer who would go to so much trouble, but this of course is typical of him."

Because of their apparent closeness to the singer, Dominic's fans feel able to make the most personal observations about every aspect of his career and personal life.

"Louise is his brick. I remember the night he told us she was pregnant," says Martina, as if discussing members of her own family. "If anything ever happened to Peter (McGlone) Dominic would be devastated. We were invited to the evening reception of Peter's son's wedding and we got word in the afternoon that Peter had had a mild stroke. The wedding went ahead, but that was a very scary time for Dominic, I think, because Pete is his soulmate on the road."

"I think he needs someone of that age group to guide him," puts in The Duchess.

The fans also feel a proprietorial right to tell Dominic exactly what they think of each of his shows and albums.

"We're very straight with Dominic and I think that's good for him," says Martina. "We don't pussyfoot with Dominic and I think he values our opinion, because at the end of the day we're not messing him about."

The adoration, however, also comes with a crushing streak of possessiveness and selfishness that the most obsessive fans seem unaware of. Many of his fans will tell you of Dominic's dedication in staying up to the small hours to meet them even when he is clearly unwell and suffering from a hacking cough. They love him for his selflessness. Yet they never question their own motives in keeping him from his rest at such times. To them, Dominic is an almost saintly figure. Always there to give to them, never needing to receive.

"Everybody here tonight has problems, be they financial, health or family," says Martina, "and he helps them to lose that for a couple of hours. He's probably got problems. But he's not a man to put that on you. You never hear any of that. You always say, 'How's Louise? How are the boys?' 'Absolutely great.'"

Martina is vehement in her criticism of Dominic's management when it comes to listening to his fans' comments and keeping them informed. In her heart, however, she is glad that the management she criticises has yet to push him any further up the ladder of success.

"Daniel has had extremely good management and PR and, unfortunately, Dominic hasn't had that," She says, "But then, if he does get higher, where would that leave us? We wouldn't have that personal touch with him."

Dominic knows the negative traits that sometimes characterise a singer's relationship with his fan base. "It's a *very* strange relationship," He agrees, gruffly. But he does nothing to distance himself from his followers.

Reporting on the internet on a show in Jersey, Gill Marseilles wrote: "I had arranged to meet Ruth and Jim in the lobby and as I was looking around for them a pair of arms went around me and a lovely kiss was planted on my cheek. I knew at once by the aftershave who it was: the man himself. . ."

In the same report, sixty-something Gill wrote of the autograph queue: "Dominic was his usual cuddly, kissy, huggy, sweet-smelling self. I had a chat and my photo taken, said goodnight and then, just as I was walking away I remembered that I had to give him a hug and a kiss from Sheila Sills. He laughed and hugged and kissed me all over again. . ."

How does Dominic's wife deal with her husband being the subject of so much over excited female attention?

"Funnily enough, I usually meet the fans in the summer time when they come to the town," says Louise Kirwan, a slim and attractive blonde who has known Dominic since childhood when they lived in the same street not far from where they live today. With a relaxed laugh, she says, "Sometimes if you're in bad form with him and they come singing his praises you feel like telling them what he's really like! Sometimes I say to Dominic when he gets up in the morning, 'If those fans could see you now!' They just think he can do no wrong, so you just have to go along with them. But I really would have no major hassles with them."

Having chosen to stay home in Omagh to raise their four sons while Dominic keeps up his relentless criss-crossing of the UK and Ireland, Louise adds, "I suppose the thing with me is I'm not jealous. That has really helped along the way. If you were jealous, I don't know if it would work.

"It also helps," says Louise, "that I have grown into the thing with Dominic. I was there when he started his first band and we grew along with it together. I wouldn't like to be somebody suddenly set into it. Like, the way Daniel O'Donnell is very famous. I would not like to be a girl set in there at this stage. The style of life takes a bit of getting used to, and the fact that I've grown with it has really helped."

Asked later about the unusual incidence of a singer taking the time to attend a fan's funeral -especially with no attempt to gain publicity from the act- Dominic says, "There are people who come to my shows that I've known a while. People have been very genuine to me. They've given me my lifestyle. They've given me a lot of their time and effort, and some people you get to know that little bit better.

"I'm not saying that you can turn up at every funeral or that you can participate at every function, but if and when you can I think it's important to do so. I knew this particular woman, Margaret Marshall, well. At The Crescent in Peterborough they were putting in new seating and people were sponsoring seats or whatever. I remember she bought a seat herself and she also bought one in my name as well. So I thought this was a real, genuine person who wanted to see me successful. I felt that in the latter days of her life, when I had contact or communication with her, the little phone call or the card sent to her meant something dear to her. So, when she did pass away, I did have the time to go.

"There was a death recently where I would have liked to have been there but, unfortunately, because of work commitments, I couldn't be. So, you can't be everywhere. But where and if possible, I would try to."

As for the question of why Martina, Fran and The Duchess have time to sit after a show talking about their hero instead of rushing to the stage door to meet him, the answer becomes clear when they eventually make their way down the stairs to the exit.

There they meet the end of a slow-moving queue that still stretches around fifty feet towards the foyer. About six feet from the end of the queue, Dominic stands in his day clothes, waiting patiently as each fan takes her turn to come forward for her ten minutes in his presence.

There's the beaming, cuddly housewife who will be at twenty-seven shows on his current tour and wants to chat as if with her best friend over the garden fence.

There's the slim, long-haired slip of a girl who steps forward to dreamily drape herself around Dominic's neck as if he were the lead singer of a teenage boy band.

There's the jolly husband and wife team, he red faced and ready with the camera while she poses with Dominic for yet another photo as if they had all just met up on holiday in Spain.

Endlessly, they come forward, one by one, each seeing him as something different: a friend, a talented son or grandson, a more interested husband, a confessor, a healer. With endless patience Dominic waits for them, with his easy smile and his tireless open arms, ready to receive each of them, young and old, with the flattering and completely selfless one-to-one attention that, in our rushed, impersonal and insincere world, they probably get from nobody else on the planet. ∎

CHAPTER THREE

My Mother's Home

" MY FATHER was a bread man," says Dominic. "He had his own van. He went door to door and I spent most of my early days with my father going in and out of people's homes delivering bread. A lot of his work would have been in the countryside around Omagh rather than in the town. So, although I am a town man, I don't consider myself to be a townie. So much so that I'm even moving to the countryside -although it's only a couple of miles along the road."

Seventy miles west of Belfast, Omagh is a provincial market town in the centre of County Tyrone, the largest county in Northern Ireland. With Dungannon and Cookstown some thirty miles to the West, and Strabane equally distant to the north, the old county town sits in the basin of a large and sparsely populated agricultural hollow where the rivers Camowen and Drumragh meet to merge and flow north as The Strule. In the highlands to the north are swathes of forest with the low, misty hump of The Sperrin Mountains visible in the distance beyond.

Dominic was not the first musician to emerge from Omagh. Among the local heroes of the show band days of the 1960s were The Plattermen, country singer Brian Coll, and Frankie

McBride who, in the summer of '67, enjoyed a Top 20 hit on the UK pop charts with *Five Little Fingers*. Dominic's roots, meanwhile, stretch north, on his mother's side, to the musical city of Derry and south, across the border, to Dublin, renowned as one of the most musical cities in the world.

"My dad's father was a soldier in the first world war," says Dominic. "He was a Dublin man, my grandfather. I didn't know him, but he was based in Omagh for a stage which is where he met my grandmother -who I do remember, because she was alive when I was born. At some stage he was shipped to the barracks in Liverpool and my father was actually born in the barracks.

"My mother is from Omagh. Her parents were City of Derry people. That's a very musical town. But she was brought up in Omagh. She was a secretary to one of the businesses in Omagh and met my father through the Boys & Girls Club in Omagh."

"Dominic was brought up with music," says his mother, Elizabeth, a feisty 76-year-old at the house she has lived in for the past 40 years and which Dominic bought for her from the council in the mid-90s, as soon as he was earning enough money to do so.

"My brothers were all musicians," says Elizabeth. "I was in the choral society. I was in choirs myself. I danced in my younger days. Although you don't know you're going to hand it on to your children."

Of Dominic's father, Elizabeth continues, "He was musical in his own way. He was very fond of country. He always listened to country. I would have been more open in my music. I used to listen to a lot of tenors, like Frank Patterson. But John always listened to country."

"He was a big fan of Irish country music, people like Brendan Shine," Dominic recalls. "That's where that side of me comes from and I'll never forget him for that. I remember one singer in particular that he had a great fondness for, who was an Omagh man as it happened, Brian Coll. Brian was more than generous, and looked after my dad and took him to many performances and shows."

The former Elizabeth Sweeny recalls how she met her husband, John Kirwan, through the Boys & Girls Club in Omagh when they were both in their early thirties: "He would be doing the office and things like that. I was in charge of the sweets and seeing everything was all right at the dances. I would have known him in the town. I'd always known who he was, but I didn't know him that well to speak to. Then there was one night when we had this carnival. It was a very wet night and my mother wasn't very well that night. I said to the priest in charge, 'I have to go home early, because my mother's not too well.' And, because it was raining, he said, 'Hold on there a second and I'll get one of the men to run you up.' It must have been John that he asked. So, he came out and said, 'I'll take you home.' Then, as we were coming out of the gate he said, 'Would you like to come for a run down the road?'

"I think that must have been how it started," smiles Elizabeth. "Then we used to have shows. Our club used to put on different musicals. We did *Showboat* and a lot of shows. John would have been the manager and I played the piano for the rehearsals."

After a year-long engagement, the pair were married on the 4th of August, 1958.

"We went to Lourdes on our honeymoon," Elizabeth recalls. "He was an asthmatic. He had been there twice before and he said to me before we got married that he wanted to go back. He said, 'Would you like to go?' So I said, 'All right, I'll go with you.' That's how we started our married life."

The newlyweds first set up home at Elizabeth's mother's house at 6, St Brigid's Terrace.

"That house no longer stands," says Dominic. "The road was re-routed, so that particular house is not there now."

"It was a small house," says Elizabeth. "My father and mother were Derry people. My father was an engine driver. He came to work in Omagh, then my mother and him came to live in Omagh. We lived in a good enough house, but at that time there was no help, so when my father died when I was only seven, my mother had to take up a smaller house."

The summer after their wedding, the couple's first daughter, Mary, was born. The following year, on the 5th of June, 1960, Elizabeth gave birth to her second child, Dominic Thomas Kirwan.

"My mother will tell you I was born in the feast of St Dominic," the singer smiles. His middle name was that of his paternal grandfather.

"It was a home birth, because my first girl, Mary, was born in hospital and at that time, if everything went well, they didn't take you into hospital for your second baby."

In June 1961, a year after Dominic was born, the Kirwans moved to larger accommodation on the newly-built Centenary Park, where his mother lives to this day.

"The housing estate was a new development in the 60s," says Dominic. "I think my mother was one of the first families on the estate. Then my grandmother moved out with them and my grandmother died in that house, within a year of coming to move there. That would have been my mother's mother, who I don't remember because I would have been maybe one year of age at the time."

At that address the Kirwans had three more daughters, Catherine, Theresa and Rosaleen, and a final son, John.

"There would have been six years between Dominic and his younger brother," says Elizabeth, "Which meant, when they were growing up they didn't have any close relationship, though they would have now."

"John and myself never really had a close relationship," Dominic agrees. "When he was 11, I was 17 and starting out in life. When he was 14, I was 20. I was a married man."

"It was a lovely quiet area," recalls Dominic's older sister, Mary. "Where we lived was always classed as a nice area. A good area to live in."

" We had the freedom to play quite openly because there were fields around before the buildings that are there now," says sister Catherine, a year Dominic's junior, who now lives in England.

"The old railway line where we used to walk to school is now the bypass," says sister Theresa, who is now also married and living in England. "I think the railway was shut down in the 60s and it was just sort of a pathway with green all around."

"We had quite an open, playful childhood," continues Catherine. "You couldn't maybe do that nowadays. I've been home quite a few times with my own children and they wouldn't have the same freedom. We used to play the old fashioned games like jail and hide and seek, where you could run into the wilds of grass and hide and play. I was quite sporty, so I used to enjoy playing badminton. We used to play that into all hours of the night when the weather was fine and the evenings were quite long."

"The boys used to be able to go down to the football field," says Theresa. "It was just a field really. They used to play football down there. Both my brothers."

"We had a three bedroom house," says Catherine. "And I was actually born in that house shortly after my mum arrived there. I was born in September 1961 and her own mother died just a fortnight after I was born. We sisters shared one room, Dominic and my other brother had the other room and my parents had the third room."

"It didn't seem crowded," says Mary, "because the rooms were bigger than they would build them now."

Even so, it was a lively household.

"It was busy and noisy when we were growing up," says Catherine.

"A lot of running about," recalls Mary. "My mother would have given out to us for throwing coats around. It was happy while my father was living."

"Music was the main thing," continues Catherine. "My father liked country and western music. My mother played the piano. She still does. We just grew up with music."

By the time his brother John was born, Dominic had already begun traditional Irish dancing lessons with Seamus Kerrigan, who remains one of the most respected teachers in the region.

"My mum actually grew up knowing him," reveals Catherine. "He was actually starting to teach the Irish dancing during the same time that she was having us children."

"My eldest girl went to dancing and I thought as he was next I would send him," recalls Elizabeth. "Of course, he didn't want to go."

Says Dominic, "I do have a memory of sitting on a wall outside my home and basically being that little boy of five or six years of age not wanting to go, but my mother and my sister persuading me."

"I would be one of those ones, with a child I never took no for an answer," confirms Elizabeth, "so I said to him, 'Go, and if you don't like it, I won't force you.'"

Seamus Kerrigan, who is currently teaching Dominic's son Barry ("and I'm not going to tell you how long I've been teaching or how old I am.."), remembers Dominic's arrival in his class, which was conducted on Saturdays at the local Christian Brothers school, which Dominic attended.

"That's where my school was born, although I'm from Donegal myself, The Christian Brothers brought me to Omagh to teach dancing in Omagh and the neighbouring vicinity. So I taught in all the towns around Tyrone."

Of his most famous pupil, Kerrigan says, "He was a podgy little fellow. But he had feet like drumsticks. He was a beautiful dancer."

"He had rhythm that very few dancers have," confirms Theresa. "What my mother always said about him was no matter what weight he had on him, because he was quite weighty when he was younger, he could still dance. He was really light on his feet."

Dominic was also a champion dancer.

"He was competing at five or six," says Kerrigan. "He was competing all his young life. Dominic won the Ulster championship and the West Tyrone Feis championship many times, and he also won in the All-Ireland dancing teams."

"I won an Ulster championship when I was about 11 or 12 years of age," says Dominic. "I was competing from the age of six or seven right up to when I was 18."

"I remember being with Daddy when he won the championship in Omagh," says Theresa. "In those days there were three adjudicators. One was at the front and two were up in the balcony, behind a board. Their job was to listen to the rhythm. At the end, the score was put up on a blackboard and each adjudicator gave their marks. There was Dominic and a fella called Shaun who were in the running for it. It was 12-6 to Dominic and 12-6 to Shaun and the last adjudicator's marks decided which won. Obviously, Dominic got the 12 and I remember my dad throwing his programme up in the air because he was so excited!"

"Irish dancing is a very competitive thing," Dominic continues. "It's probably even more competitive today because of *Riverdance* and *Lord Of The Dance*. But even at that time it was something that all mums and dads seemed to take a pride in their kids going in and being well groomed and well rehearsed.

"I was one of those guys that wasn't as well rehearsed as a lot of them," Dominic confesses. "But because of my natural ability I just seemed to be able to dance. It wasn't a problem. There were times when I won and probably surprised myself."

"I wouldn't say Dominic was competitive," agrees Theresa. "I would say he enjoyed it. He enjoyed the social side of it. He had a talent which he knew he had, but if he had wanted to do more with it, he would have had to practise more and put more into it. But he did enough to win."

Asked if dancing lessons were a financial sacrifice for his family, Dominic replies, "My family did their best for me. My dad was just a working-class man. It would have been a big cost between costumes and travelling and then, of course, there were my sisters in it as well. But they were a typical working-class family. They believed in their kids. They brought their kids into the world and they wanted to give their kids the best they could and they would have sacrificed a lot of things themselves for us. So it was a big cost, but it never seemed to show too much."

What was Master Kerrigan like?

"Strict!" Exclaims Theresa, and bursts out laughing. "Strict but good. We were terrified of him. You were terrified if you made a mistake while you were on that stage."

Elizabeth Kirwan describes Kerrigan as a "good influence" on her children. "He didn't take any answering back from children. He taught them a lot of manners. You always knew a Kerrigan dancer when you saw them."

"Seamus was a disciplinarian," says Dominic, "but he showed a lot of respect for the kids as well. He was a father figure whenever we'd all head off to competitions. I think our parents were very aware of that and very happy to have him around."

One of Dominic's fellow dancers was a quick-witted blonde called Louise McHugh who lived in the same street as him and who, by the time Dominic was twenty, would become Louise Kirwan.

"He lived in Number 8 and I lived in Number 29. So, from the top bedroom of our house, I could see his house," laughs Louise. "But he was able to sneak out of the bottom of the park, and I could sneak out. There were two entrances, so you could still sneak out."

Prophetically, four years before they were married in church, Dominic and Louise were married in one of Seamus Kerrigan's *song scenas*.

"I put a wedding scene in at the end," Kerrigan remembers with a smile. "The song was *The Bells Of St Mary*. Dominic was the leading boy and the girl he married was the leading girl. That's when he was about 16. And the girl he 'married' was Louise, his wife."

Louise, like Dominic, was one of the few dancers to remain pupils of Kerrigan's until their late teens. But she admits, "Seamus and I had a wee fall out at one stage. I remember I was up crying to Dominic saying, 'Master Kerrigan says not to come back to dance!'"

Despite his strictness, however, Kerrigan was respected and liked by his pupils.

"Not only was he a great teacher," says Dominic, "he was also a great ambassador in many ways to travel with." After her brief falling out, Louise recalls "I went back to the dancing and he maybe ignored me for a few weeks. But he came to our wedding and we're still great friends. He's a lovely man."

As well as travelling throughout Ireland, Irish dancing afforded Dominic, his sisters and his future wife their first taste of overseas travel, to take part in festivals in Scotland, France and Norway.

"If it hadn't been for the dancing, I would never have got out of Omagh," says Louise. "We'd go to festivals. Mr Kerrigan would put on a minibus and you'd all pay a little bit to the minibus and take your packed lunch. So, as well as getting you out of town, it got you a little bit of independence. Apart from that, you'd never have been away without your mother and that kind of thing. When we went to Norway it was the first time I'd ever been on a plane. It was a brilliant experience."

Dominic remembers Bergen and days out in Oslo. "The Fjords. I can remember the scenery and the types of housing that were there. I remember being taken away up into the mountains to a residential type of home. As a family we were not in the financial bracket to have any major holidays or such, so Irish dancing got me travelling."

"We had a marvellous two weeks in Norway and a wonderful reception," recalls Kerrigan. "I remember one night. . . I had thirty young people with me, so I picked six of them to give a special display at this particular function. It was a very important venue and Dominic and his present wife were among the six I picked."

Were Dominic and Louise boyfriend and girlfriend at that stage?

"Well, I would never have encouraged that," Kerrigan says firmly. "It might have been, unknown to me, but I don't think there was really. I just picked them because of their ability at singing and dancing."

Louise, however, remembers things differently. "We were," she confesses, adding, "Mr Kerrigan knew, and at that time he didn't like relationships within the dancing." With a laugh, she adds, "He had his way of separating you!"

"As a teacher I didn't encourage that sort of thing," continues Kerrigan. "I was interested in getting them interested in the dancing. I didn't want them interested in each other. I had to be very responsible for them. I had to have very strict discipline."

Also in Norway was Dominic's younger sister, Theresa, and she reveals that Dominic could be just as protective as Master Kerrigan.

"He was always the big brother, making sure you weren't up to any. . . meeting boyfriends, or anything like that!"

Having been successful in competitions, did Dominic ever express a desire to take his dancing further by turning professional?

"No," says Kerrigan, "not such as *Lord Of The Dance*. There was nothing like that in our day. You just went on to become an

Ulster champion or an All-Ireland champion, and if you were interested enough, you went on and took a teacher's examination and became a teacher. But Dominic wasn't motivated in that way."

However, Seamus maintains that, "The one thing that has helped him in his present (music) thing is his Irish dancing, because it always had great appeal. As in any production, no matter how good the singing is, it takes the dancing to give it that lift."

As well his talent for dancing, Dominic naturally liked to sing, although in the early days he tended to hide his light under a bushel.

"You'd never hear Dominic singing in the house." remembered Theresa, "I think he was quite shy in those days."

Dominic explains, "Where I come from, and it probably happens everywhere but I can only relate to my own area, you were always trying to be aware of not trying to be the up-front guy all the time. Not wanting to be called the big headed type character. So I think I played it down a lot. I was the sort of guy who thought, well, I want to do what I do and I enjoy what I do, it's a natural talent, but I don't need anybody cutting me to pieces. That probably played a big part in my life then and maybe some of it still does today."

Dominic was ten when his mother was first told by one of his teachers at the local Christian Brothers' school that her son had a beautiful voice. "There was a *feis* on at the time and the teacher said, 'What we want you to do is go along and listen to him.' I remember telling his daddy and he said, 'If you go, don't let him see you, because if he sees you he's not going to sing.' So I had to go down and stand at the back. But I remember he won, and from there on he was in competitions during the year and he would have been winning these competitions.

"As he grew older, he used to lead the singing in the church on a Sunday morning," says Elizabeth.

"Those memories are always going to be there," Dominic says fondly. "I still go to the same church. I've done solo performances and I've done parts in the choirs. My family would have been very much part of those things. My mum, at 76, is still part of the local choir.

"We, being part of the younger generation, were probably involved in the first folk choirs in my local church. It's something I would do again. If I had the time on my hands I would even join the choir again, but unfortunately I don't have the time to give to it."

As was common at the time, Dominic's local Sacred Heart church had its own folk group of which Dominic was an enthusiastic part.

Theresa remembers that many folk groups were set up after Pope John Paul visited Ireland. "Paul Pritchard who is the church organist and quite a genius in his own right ran the folk group. It tended to comprise two families, the Pritchards and the Kirwans.

" It was a more modern thing to do. The music was more exciting, really. For example, you could take *Lord Of The Dance* and just jazz it up and play it in church. It was all harmonised. It was for young people."

Dominic also participated in local amateur musicals ."He was in *Joseph*," says Elizabeth. "He was in *Jesus Christ Superstar*. His wife took part in them as well."

In fact, Dominic's whole family were musically gifted.

"Every year we used to compete as a family in the local *feis*," says Catherine. "It was quite hilarious, really, because we used to have five minutes practice before the main event, then we'd go up and win the competition."

As a child and young teenager, however, Dominic was never aware of a conscious ambition to be a star.

"I suppose some people might find that strange. I've never once sat down and thought, 'This is what I'm going to do, I'm going to be a professional singer.' Yet, at the same time, I was always taking part in competitions or doing as much as possible to be seen or heard, so I suppose there was a little driving force behind me. I had that inkling that, 'This is what you need to do.' As for sitting down and saying, 'Here's a five year plan and by the end of that I'm going to be doing something. . .' that was never done."

Between his dancing, singing and a passion for Gaelic football, Dominic had less time for school, which he left at the age of 16.

"He was a clever boy," recalls Seamus Kerrigan. "He was university material, one of the Christian Brothers used to tell me. But then he didn't continue in school."

"He was a bright enough fella at school," remembers his mother. "But I suppose with his dancing and football and things like that, he wouldn't have been a great fella for his studying. He didn't want to study too much, let's put it that way."

Told that some of his teachers referred to him as potential university material, Dominic chuckles and says, "Well, my mother will tell you that. She would say, particularly at school meetings, the main gist of the conversation would have been, 'The man's capable, but he's just not working.' That had been said about me on a few occasions. I suppose my interests were everywhere but school."

Today Dominic claims: "I've never been bad at maths. If anything, that's probably something that's stayed with me, because I've had to do it. History was one of my better subjects. English was not one of my greater ones. That's something that's been detrimental to me over the years. I find at times I would have difficulty with certain aspects of the English language. I probably understand a lot more about it today, but I didn't do enough of it at the time".

As for music, he found theory difficult. "I can see my own

son now working at music and I know the approach is completely different. I did take it on for O Level and go so far with it but. . . the books were too thick!" Dominic laughs. "That's the honest truth of it. The books were too thick!"

In terms of instruments, Dominic learned to play the trumpet at school, although it's not something he continued with in adult life. His biggest regret is that he didn't learn to play his mother's instrument, the piano.

"Two of my sisters and myself went to piano lessons," says Catherine. I think Dominic wished his mum had sent him to the piano lessons instead of the Irish dancing."

"I do that," Dominic confirms. "I still say to my boys, 'Learn piano. Have piano as an instrument.' But it didn't click with me and I didn't go that way. There were maybe times when I didn't even want to hear the piano being played. I don't know why."

Did Dominic get into much trouble at school?

"I suppose I was no angel," He shrugs. "There were situations of running down corridors and being pulled in by a teacher -the headmaster he is now, in fact, but he wasn't then- and being taken in front of a class of sixth formers and spanked on me behind with a blackboard duster when I was only in the second year. I don't have any really bad memories of school. I don't remember not wanting to go to school."

Dominic's final years at grammar school, however, were not his happiest.

Asked if Dominic enjoyed his school days, older sister Mary answers with a firm, "No. I think the word now is bullying. He wouldn't let my parents know. He pleaded with them to let him leave school. the weren't happy about it, but in the end he got his way. He regrets that now. But that's just the way it was. Now, he'll talk to his boys about bullying. It's more open than it was then."

"He never said to me about bullying or anything like that," recalls Elizabeth. "I didn't know until after he left school that a bit of bullying went on. It was Theresa that told me, och, a long time after the both of them had left school. At the time he had said to Theresa, "Don't tell Mammy." So I never knew. He kept it to himself. I suppose he thought I'd be annoyed and maybe I would head up to the school or something – which I suppose any mother would do. Although he did talk to me about it not long ago when we were talking about bullying at school. I said to him, "Would you have been bullied at school?" He said, "Oh, I was, but I soon finished that.." He said, "I got the fella once and that was that." He didn't say much about it.

"It was because he was fat," Elizabeth explains. "When he went to grammar school, he put on a lot of weight. Then, as he grew older, he started to lose the weight."

Of Dominic's decision to leave school at 16, Elizabeth admits, "I was a wee bit annoyed at the time. Maybe a year afterwards he regretted it himself."

Dominic, however, already had a job to go to.

"My first job was with a guy called Declan O'Neill and I was with Declan for the next seven to eight years. There is still a company in my home town called O'Neill Motor Factors, but it was bought out by another company."

He first met O'Neill through the St Enda's Gaelic Football Club, while still at school.

"I was a youth member of the committee and Declan was the chairman of the club. In the latter half of my 15th year I went and worked for the Easter holidays with him, then I worked the summer holidays. Over the summer holidays he offered me a job, so I stayed with him."

"I had a business both in Strabane and Omagh and Dominic worked in both places for me as a counter assistant and van salesman," recalls O'Neill. "My business was in wholesale, selling spare parts to the retail sector."

Of Dominic's football skills, O'Neill says, "He was a goalkeeper. He showed a lot of promise in his earlier days. He would have been a great youth member of the club, too, in terms of organising things."

In particular, O'Neill remembers Dominic representing St Enda's in Irish dancing and singing competitions between the Gaelic football clubs. "He would have won heaps of awards in that respect. He was very strong voiced. He would have been a great singer of the old traditional Irish ballads. The *Danny Boy*s and Mountains of Mourne, for example."

Dominic also supplemented his income working shifts behind the bar at the football club. Perhaps one reason he felt the need to leave school and bring home a wage was that by the time he entered his teens, his father had finally been forced by ill health to give up work. He was just 47 at the time.

Four years later, when he was just 17, Dominic became the oldest male in the house.

"My dad was an unwell man all his life. My grandmother tells the story that when he was very young he had no ill health at all for about three years. It was only when he was three years old that he took to ill health through asthma. But he fought it very, very hard. There were times when I did see him suffer a lot. But he was a grafter. He was always on time. He was very clean with his work. He was very proud of his people that he served his bread to. He would have looked after them to the final minute.

"I spent a lot of years with him on his local bread run," Dominic continues, "The main thing I remember is his honesty. His honesty not alone for himself, but for his work. His loyalty to his company, which I suppose is the most important thing for a worker and which I think is not as popular now as it was in our parents' day.

"He totally cared for his people. If he was running short in his van and it was Christmas Eve, that man would have worked 'til the last minute on Christmas Eve night, even if it meant him going into the shops to buy the products so that he could at least serve his customers.

"He enjoyed a laugh," Dominic continues. "He was a very generous and sincere man. He was also a member of the St Vincent D'Paul society in Ireland, which is a charitable organisation to look after the poor.

"He told us many stories about his youthful days when, although he was not an able bodied man himself, he was involved with the local Boys and Girls Club when it started up in Omagh. He very much enjoyed athletics and drove the athletes to the different venues. So, he was an active man."

Taking a deep breath, Dominic remembers the day that his father passed away.

"It was sudden. I remember it well. It was a Tuesday afternoon. I was a young boy coming home from work. I remember seeing an ambulance sitting outside the front door. Going in. A priest sitting with him. He said, 'I'm OK. I just had a wee turn and they're gonna take me to Dungannon.'

"My father had never been in hospital before. This was all new, because he had fought every situation that he could fight. But he was taken off to hospital. He didn't let me go, because I was only driving a little at the time. He said, 'You're only young. Sure, you can come up and see me tomorrow night.'

"So I brought my mother up the following evening. He had a bit of a problem passing water. They had to do a catheter job on him. But once that was done he was relaxed. He was smoking his pipe. He insisted that I go home early, because it was one of the longer journeys I had done at the time."

A few hours after Dominic and his mother returned home, however, they received a phone call to say his father had taken a turn for the worse.

"Our neighbour got the phone call because we didn't have a phone at home at the time. They insisted that they took us back to the hospital and those are two people I will be eternally grateful to, Gerry and Bridie Donnelly. Funnily enough, they're neighbours of mine now. They moved from the estate and they live about four doors from where I live."

Taking another deep breath, Dominic resumes, "When we arrived at the hospital my mother was taken for a cup of tea. I just wanted to go and see my dad. I wouldn't have been there more than ten or fifteen minutes and he just passed away in his sleep."

Catherine remembers the night her father died. "Dominic was by the bedside. It was early morning and I turned over to see a figure sitting on the side of the bed. It was Dominic, just sort of staring at us, my sister and myself. He woke us up to tell us the news.

"They said on the death certificate it was chronic bronchitis and emphysema. As we were growing up we knew he had chest problems, but he was the sort of man who was quite stubborn and he wouldn't go for treatment. So there could have been a lot done for him -or there could be nowadays."

"Dominic always had a great relationship with his father," says Elizabeth. "They would have watched the football together."

"Daddy idolised Dominic and Dominic idolised Daddy," says Theresa.

"Dominic really loved him," Mary agrees.

"He was a big chunk taken out of my life," says Dominic. "I suppose you never miss the water 'til the well runs dry. My father had more to do with the way I'm shaped today than any other person.

"I know I missed him badly and have done over the years. I still do. There's times when I just wished to God he was there and I could have asked him a question or two. But I've got this faith thing. I think there are people around you, and maybe his spirit's with me at times. Maybe that's what made me get on with life."

Theresa shares this view. "I'd say to this day Daddy's still very much with Dominic. Daddy's always talked about within the family. He's 23 years dead now and we still bring him into conversations.

"I'd say Dominic was one of the luckier ones because he had probably the best relationship with Daddy, because Dominic would go out on the bread van with him. They would have had conversations and Daddy talked to him like a little man. Dominic knew more about Daddy than we would, really. I think Dominic had that privilege where we didn't."

Looking back, many years later, Dominic's wife, Louise says, "I think Dominic felt that his father was torn away from him at the time when he needed him. And at a time, maybe, when he could do things with him. He'd always have loved to have been able to go out and have a pint with his father. Like when our son Lee was 18, he had his first drink with Dominic. Dominic always said that was one of the things he always regretted not being able to do with his own father." ■

CHAPTER FOUR

Dom in Las Vegas

U NTIL the bomb that made Omagh international news in the summer of 1988, Dominic's hometown was relatively unscathed by the troubles that ravaged Northern Ireland throughout the years of his youth. The largest previous incident in the town was in May 1973 when five off-duty soldiers were killed by an IRA bomb at the Knock-na-Moe Castle Hotel – a venue where Dominic would later meet his manager Charlie McBrien and personal assistant Peter McGlone. Although the spectre of violence was never far from daily life in the province, the Kirwan children did not feel especially oppressed by the conflict, even as they grew into teenagers and wanted to enjoy their freedom.

"I could never understand English people saying, 'Oh God, I couldn't go out over there,' says Dominic's younger sister, Theresa, who now lives on the mainland. "We never thought that way. There was the odd bomb or shooting. But it never stopped you going out. You weren't frightened. It never stopped you from getting on with things.

"If there was a bomb in the town we'd go outside and guess where the bomb was. But, at that time, nobody was hurt much. It tended to be at night when the shops were closed."

Recalling his teenage years, Dominic says, "The 70s were a very, very hard time in Northern Ireland. It was a case of watching your step. You had to be careful about where you were going, what dances you were going to, who you travelled with, what company you kept. But it's like that today, in many respects. Only maybe it's the drug world today.

"So it was a hard time. But because of the way I lived my life with my schooling, my dancing and my singing, a lot of it was kept away from me."

The Kirwan family were, however, directly touched by the Troubles.

"My dad's mother lived in a place called Artizan Terrace," says Dominic. "She lived alone and she would have been an early-to-bed person and, in the early days of the Troubles, the local police barracks was built more or less in front of that street."

"She got bombed out of her house a few times when the police station was targeted," says Theresa. "She used to come and stay with us. I think twice it happened, and the last time she couldn't go back again."

"We had to get her out of the house and when we got back it was in ruins and totally devastated," says Dominic. "She never went back after that. She lived with us for, I think, a year or two until she died."

Although the Kirwans were active churchgoers, their children were not brought up in an atmosphere of religious intolerance.

"As children I think our parents didn't want us to live in fear," says Theresa. "I'm proud of the way our parents brought us up to believe that there's good on every side. We certainly weren't brought up believing in one thing. It was quite open in that way. It was good ."

"I was never brought up to be a bigoted person," confirms Dominic. "I respect all aspects of life and I do respect, actually, traditions as well. I think everybody should respect each other's traditions. It's important that all traditions are looked at. But, how to hate someone because they were another religion. . ." The singer shakes his head with a deep frown. "I can't fathom that at all."

With the loss of his father at such an impressionable age, Dominic could have been forgiven for going off the rails as a teenager.

"There's times I probably should have," he admits. But he adds with a sigh, "I think I was too sensible. I love a laugh and a joke and all the rest of it, but I'm probably too serious about things, you know? That's the part of me that I wish to God would lighten up a bit more. But I'm forty years of age now. I still enjoy a laugh. I still enjoy company and all the rest, but there's a very serious side to me, and it sometimes annoys me."

Of teenage bad habits, Dominic confesses, "I would have smoked, like a lot of young guys at school. I never liked smoking, yet it's that thing that you did. I gave up cigarettes when I was 20 or 21, and I never looked back. I wouldn't put one in my mouth now if you paid me.

"I wouldn't have taken a lot of drink. I was never a crazy drinking guy. I didn't really drink until I was about 18."

If Dominic displayed few signs of teenage angst, it was at least in part due to the fact that he had to grow up quickly and assume the role of man of the house.

"At that point it was quite difficult for my mum," says Dominic's sister Catherine. "She had six children under the age of 18. I was 16 and Dominic was 17 when my father died, so he was more or less the figurehead."

"I remember him just being there for us after Daddy died," agrees Theresa. "I think the rest of us had him to fall back on."

"It's funny," says Catherine, "as sisters, now that we look back on it, we would always talk and say, well, 'Who gave Dominic the support? Who was there for him?'"

"Dominic definitely took on the role of the father in the

house," says Theresa. "He was always looked upon and relied upon. If decisions were to be made, they would be made when Dominic came home."

"But Dominic was starting to take that role over before my father died," points out younger brother John. "When they were deciding something, if something had to be bought, my parents would have said, 'Well, let's see what the big fella thinks.' So they would have brought him into more adult conversation and given him more responsibility even before my father died. If there were problems with the younger ones in the house my mother consulted him."

Louise, Dominic's girlfriend of the time and now his wife, says of his dedication to his family in the wake of his father's death, "He had to be there for his mum. He was the fatherly figure. Even as far as going out to mass on a Sunday, Dominic would have driven his family there."

Did Dominic feel that a heavy burden of responsibility had been placed on his young shoulders because of his father's death?

"It was a confusing time, there's no doubt about that. I probably did feel I had to take over. But that time, between 17 and 20, when I got married, seemed to go so fast. I obviously looked for other things. I looked for a relationship. I probably did feel the burden of it, but probably didn't deal with it too well."

"He was very protective," says Theresa, adding with a laugh, "He was a pain as well! I tried to avoid him sometimes. Especially with boyfriends. You were just gonna get hassle from him. Not hassle in a bad way. It was in a brotherly way."

Even older sister Mary had her suitors vetted by Dominic, commenting, "And I was a year older than him – not that that seemed to matter!"

Dominic sighs. "That was the typical thing then. When my dad was alive I would have been sent out to local dances and clubs; watch this and watch the rest. OK, you do it, but I look back today and if I was asked to do it today I'd say forget it. But what do you know when you're 14, 15 years of age and you've got an older sister?"

As his father knew he was not a well man, does Dominic feel his father might have spent their time together on the bread run grooming him to look after the family in the event that he wouldn't be around to do so?

"I've never thought of it like that, but it makes sense, there's no doubt about that." says the singer. "He taught me a fair bit of independence. Although we were a very close family and my mother did everything for us, and it wasn't until I started going out with Louise that I started to become a more independent fella in terms of having to do things for myself. Since then, I've always been an independent guy."

Aside from responsibility to his family, Dominic's main priority in his late teens was music. In particular, he threw himself into his first band, The Melody Boys, which he formed with his best friend, Barry Bradley, whom he knew through his Irish dancing lessons.

"Barry was very much into music and very much into country music," says Dominic. "He was probably into more country music than I was. We were members of the local boys club and there were a bunch of lads that wanted to play in a band."

Bradley, who went to primary school with Dominic, although they later attended different schools, remembers: "There were a few friends of mine at school, Martin Bradley, who was no relation, Joe Cuthbertson and a wee fella called Chris Clarke. We were just messing about at school and we decided to put a band together. I knew what talent Dominic had and I suggested to the lads that we get him in. They were a bit reluctant at the time, probably because the only time we would have heard Dominic was singing in the chapel and things like that. In those days we were trying to do covers of pop songs and it was maybe, like, he might not be suitable for that kind of stuff."

As soon as Dominic sang with the guys, however, there were no more questions about his ability to front the group.

"His talent really shone," says Bradley. "It was also the hard work he put in. His determination to do things and get things. Even though in the early days a couple of us would have had full-time jobs, he would have been the fella who would have put money up for everybody. Or, he would put his own money back in to make sure the boys would have gear. If they wanted something they'd get it, you know?"

"I just seemed to have that little driving force within me to be able to organise it," says Dominic. "To be able to arrange equipment and maybe get halls booked. That was always something I did from a very early age."

The name The Melody Boys came with a pedigree.

According to Bradley, "There was a very famous band around Tyrone in the early 60s and one of the names of the band was The Plattermen. I'm sure they were called The Melody Boys before they took the names The Platters and then The Plattermen. That would have been a good ten or twenty years before us. So this name came up from the past that really hadn't been used."

Recalling the band's early days of music making, Bradley says, "I remember walking into a music shop one day and I don't think we even knew what we were going to play. So I looked up and I saw this shiny bass guitar and I thought, 'I'm gonna play that.' Somebody else would say, 'Well I'll play that other one.' That's when I took up bass because I had been playing the ordinary guitar up until then.

"We rehearsed in the Boys Club in part of the Christian Brothers school," Bradley continues. "They used to have all sorts of wee dances there. There would have been a couple of bands there, rehearsing in different parts of the hall."

The musical style of the band evolved around the central force of Dominic's voice.

"You might say you wanted to do cover versions of the pop music of the time," says Bradley, "and some of them suited Dominic's voice, but some of them wouldn't suit at all. So that's when he would start doing ballad songs. *The Town I Loved So Well*. *Noreen Bawn* was even sung in the early days. It was a really big attraction for people to hear him singing those types of songs.

"At that time, Joe Dolan would have been really big on the go and Dominic's voice would have been suited to that type of material. So we would have honed in and said, 'Right, if you can do this type of stuff let's do it.' And when we did it sounded pretty good."

Naturally, there were creative differences and, occasionally, feelings between the testosterone-charged young men ran high.

"My memories of that time are very vivid," says Dominic. "I remember the first drummer that we had, a guy called Joe Cuthbertson who, thankfully, I am great friends with today. Joe was a great wee drummer. But I suppose everybody had that little bit of aggression. Everybody wanted to be getting better. I remember one day at rehearsals I was trying to organise a Status Quo medley or something and Joe was a bit over the top in his drumming. I kept saying, 'Look, stop drumming there for a moment.' But he wouldn't do it. I lost my head and rather than go round the kit, I went *through* the kit.

"Joe just packed up his kit and left there and then. My next drummer, Jay McGaghran, happened to be standing there. He was a guy that was just friendly with us. I said, 'Are you a drummer?' He said, 'I do a bit of drumming.' 'Have you a kit?' 'No, I don't.' So, we went to a local music shop and I did the whole business of organising a kit. Then he became my drummer for the next few years and, not only that, he then became my first sound engineer when I got my Ritz deal."

The Melody Boys' first gigs were arranged through the Boys Club. Dominic's boss, Declan O'Neill, provided a van and the band quickly became a popular booking for pubs and social functions.

"We played everything," says Dominic. "Country. Irish. music from the 60s. Whatever was happening in the 70s. . ."

With a laugh, Bradley remembers Dominic's over-eagerness to get to their first gig.

"Dominic came in and I had my amplifier sitting on my speaker. He said, 'Are you ready?' 'I'm ready, aye.' So he lifted the amplifier to head out the door with it. It would have been quite a heavy piece of amplification. The only problem was the leads were still plugged into the wall, so everything kinda came with him as he headed out the door!"

What did Dominic's family think of The Melody Boys?

"When he started in bands I wasn't very much for it," admits his mother, Elizabeth. "I used to say to him, 'I'd prefer it if you had a nine to five job. But he had this thing and if I'd stopped him I'd have been the worst in the world and he would have never forgiven me.

"Then, when he was starting out and trying to make it a wee bit, things weren't going too well for him. I remember him coming in to me one day and saying, 'I don't see any light at the end of the tunnel, Mummy, maybe some day I'll have to give it up.' I remember saying to him then, 'Well, there's a saying, if at first you don't succeed, try, try again.' So he went on ahead. I have to say, everything he's got, he's worked hard for."

Theresa remembers, "If they were playing locally, we used to go and watch them play. They were probably one of the better little groups around town."

Catherine adds, "They'd do Smokie songs like *Needles & Pins*. All those old 70s songs."

"When I was 13 or 14 I would have heard them playing in the

Coach Inn," says John. "I used to help them lift their gear up. And they were a good band. I remember them doing a Beatles medley: *I Want To Hold Your Hand, All my loving, Get Back* -stuff like that. A bit of ELO. Dave Edmunds -*Queen Of Hearts*. Nick Lowe -*I Knew The Bride When She Used To Rock'n'Roll*. Dominic's big thing in those days, probably still is, was *Noreen Bawn*. Even then you'd see people going mad for it. They'd love to hear him singing it, even 20 years ago in his own town."

One of the most important gigs of Dominic's early career was at the Knock-na-Moe Castle Hotel in Omagh. The hotel manager was Peter McGlone who many years later would become Dominic's driver and assistant on the road. The hotel owner, Michael Ward, who was also a painting and decorating contractor, took over Dominic's sponsorship, providing him with a van, and Charlie McBrien, who was booking acts for the hotel, became Dominic's manager.

Of the Knock-na-Moe Castle, Dominic admits: "I always talk about my break as being the 7th of January, 1989, when I got my recording contract with Ritz, but, looking back, that was the start of it all, there.

"I'd known of Charlie McBrien a long time," says Dominic. "He was a local character who had managed bands for many, many years. He'd been involved with people like Larry Cunningham and The Clipper Carlton Show Band. He'd been an agent for booking dance halls in the show band era. He even managed Philomena Begley before I came along. Brendan Quinn was another.

"He was a very cautious man," Dominic adds. "He had tramped the roads through the show band era and got to know the business very, very well. Definitely, by the time I started to work with him, he came with a very wise background to him. We had our ups and downs as any management system would have. But I have to say that now he's gone from life he was a man who would have been very influential in getting me the breaks in the business. He became very much like a father figure around me on the road and I believe he felt like that as well. He was very protective. But, at the same time, if he was difficult to work with it was because if he made a decision that was the way things had to be.

"I can remember this particular statement that Larry Cunningham once said about him. 'If you owed Charlie a pound he would never let you away with it. He would never do you on a pound. And if you got on the wrong side of him you knew about it.' In other words, things would have closed down on you very quickly in the business. Larry summed Charlie up very well in those three statements. He was very much about fairness and honesty. If you worked for him you got paid. If you owed him you paid him and, at the end of the day, you didn't cross him."

It was through Charlie McBrien's contacts that Dominic made his first appearances on the mainland.

Dominic recalls, "We did weekend packages of maybe playing an Irish centre in Leeds and an Irish centre in Manchester. We were playing the National in London and maybe a few other smaller clubs in London, just to get into London. It was a great thing for a local lad to say. 'Well, where are you playing?' 'We're playing in London, you know?"

Not that there was anything glamorous about Dominic's early trips across the water.

"I remember breakdowns on the way home, trying to get to the boat in the older vans that we used to have. There was one particular incident. We had a battered old diesel Transit van. We were on our way back to the boat and we broke down just about Junction 19 on the M6. One of the boys in the band, Chris Clarke, or as we all knew him, Dip, had a bit of a mechanical head on him and he realised what had happened. We'd broken two injectors in the engine. So he leaned over the engine and grabbed the two injector pipes and held them together so that I could drive with my head hanging out of the window -on the M6 of all places! At Junction 19 we got off and found a small garage and got the pipes made. Then we got to the boat -and we broke down again."

Strangely enough, adds Dominic, "I was to meet the people that have sponsored me since 1991 more or less at that same junction. So, Junction 19 on the M6 has always been something special to me."

It was also while in London that Dominic spied another glimpse of the future.

"I remember being in the National Ballroom about 1985, seeing a poster for Daniel O'Donnell, and I'd never heard of him. I remember asking Gerry Smithers, who ran The National, about him and Gerry saying to me, 'He's gonna be really big. This guy's gonna do well.' And we look back and he has done well."

By that time Dominic was a married man and father, having married Louise on the 29th of December, 1980, at their local Sacred Heart church. Given the nature of his musical repertoire today Dominic's legion of swooning fans might imagine that his proposal was a romantic occasion with flowers, candlelight and maybe even a song. But the singer says gruffly, "No. I was a very natural and normal kid coming off the streets, so it wasn't like that as such. I would believe in a bit of romance, but I maybe wasn't as romantic then. I can't really see myself as being the romantic type."

Asked if Dominic's proposal was romantic, Louise bursts out laughing before saying, "No, not really. He's romantic enough now, but not then. He'd always remember birthdays and anniversaries. He'd always have sent flowers."

How did Dominic's mother react to news of his forthcoming wedding?

"Well, I only heard a short while before!" She smiles: "It sort of came as a shock to me, because you think you're going to keep your sons. However, he did well for himself and Louise has been a good mother to his children."

"When we first got married, we didn't have a lot between us, so we actually lived with Louise's sister for about six months," says Dominic. "That was in the area of the town where I live now, the Tamlaght Road region."

On the 25th of June, 1981, Louise gave birth to the first of Dominic's four sons, Lee who, though leaner in the face, would grow up to bear an uncanny resemblance to his father. How did Dominic adapt to fatherhood?

"Well, it probably came on a lot faster than I thought," says the singer. "Louise was pregnant when we got married. But it's something you switch into. You knuckle down. You get on with life. You realise where you are, you get settled and you have your family.

"But the music industry was always around me and it was always taking me away from that. So I was in and out all the time, but doing the best that I could do."

Looking back on the effect of his career on his relationship with his children Dominic says, "I suppose Lee must have been nine or ten when I got my record contract. Colm would have been six or seven and Barry was only three or four. So, really, my family has grown up with me in the music industry. It's not something they don't know about. They know everything about it -how we all lived. They've seen their lifestyle change with it and, in all fairness to them, they've had more comfortable surroundings than I would have had as a kid."

Dominic and Louise's first real marital home was a rented three-bedroom house at 3 Glenelly Gardens.

"It was in an area called Strathroy which, from where we lived, would have been maybe two miles away," says Louise. "It was a completely different area, which we didn't like at all -I think just because it was a different area of the town. It was so totally different. And, at that stage, I actually worked in our end of town."

At least, having the privacy of their own home was an improvement on staying with relatives.

"I think you feel like you're over crowding the place," says Louise of the months she and Dominic lived with her sister Valerie and her husband Brendan. "We felt at the time it was better than moving in with one of our mums. At least we'd have someone of our own age group and they'd be more understanding. As well as that, Valerie and Brendan own a furniture shop in the town, so they were out all day, really, and you had the house to yourself nearly all day. But when the baby cried, you'd still feel like, 'Oh, my God. We're in the way here.'"

When The Melody Boys eventually went their separate ways, giving in to the need to raise families and earn livings, Barry Bradley, who had served an apprenticeship as an engineer, moved to London in search of gainful employment. He lives there to this day and in the evenings fronts his own band The Breeze. Looking back on his first band with Dominic, he says, "I remember playing Donegal the night before I left. But we had so many good times. The band kinda went from being a pub band to touring Ireland. That was really exciting for youngsters like ourselves. We had some good times along the way."

Good times that Dominic was far from ready to give up. With the demise of The Melody Boys, he continued to front a number of bands, including a short stint with a 50s style rock'n'roll outfit called Hi-De-Hi, which took its name from the highly popular television sitcom set in a holiday camp.

"The band was run by a family in Dungannon called The Corrigan family," recalls Dominic. "Before Hi-De-Hi I was in small groups in town. One group was called The Entertainers, which I fronted with two brothers, Paddy and Shaun Phillips and Noelle McCaffery. Again, it was a covers band. Any of the bands I was in, our main work was that local pub thing or, after that, that local wedding, dinner dance thing. That's the work I was doing, within a 50 to 100 mile radius of home."

Dominic's younger brother, John, acted as his roadie for a while in the mid-80s before embarking on his own musical career. Still playing semi-professionally today, as a solo performer around Omagh, John recalls, "He used to have an old Transit van that leaked when it rained. So, if you had a long journey, you could get fairly wet. The band had an old sofa in the back to sit on. So it was not very glamorous touring. And a lot of this, I can remember, was in winter. I don't remember very many nice summer nights.

"Sometimes he would head off to a place like Dublin and the agreement was that you could come and play and you'd get the door -and ten people might turn up. But he'd play anyway. Gradually the thing built up. A few more, a few more. It was a hard slog, but he was hungry. He had a determination to succeed and, to me, even then he had a bit of an edge over some performers. Some people seem born for the stage and he certainly was."

Even in the days of The Melody Boys, it was apparent that Dominic was the attraction that people came to see and, as a reflection of his growing reputation, even that band quickly became billed as Dominic Kirwan & The Melody Boys. There was, however, a time in certain parts of Northern Ireland, when Dominic's name was considered a liability.

"We had a band called Don and Las Vegas," chuckles the singer who, at the time sported a moustache that would have made a kebab shop owner envious. He grows more serious, however, as he explains, "There was a guy who looked after me for a while called Kevin Duffy and one of the problems we were having. . . it's a stupid thing in Northern Ireland, but it did happen. . . my name Dominic would be very much a Catholic name and some people felt it was too strong for certain parts of Northern Ireland. So, rather than Dominic, we went Don.

"I always used to think it was really stupid," the singer continues, "and I always had in the back of my head, 'I'm gonna prove it's wrong.' I'm not sectarian in any way and I always kept thinking to myself, 'I'll prove these people wrong,' and that you can be who you are and you must be taken for yourself. So, when I got the Ritz deal, I made the decision that it was going to be Dominic Kirwan and I was going to be known for who I was and what I was."

Of playing Northern Ireland's trouble spots, like the Falls and Ardoyne, John recalls, "I think Dominic went to places in the Shankhill. Both sides of the house. Those were rough days, although if you were a musician you were let in. But some of the places he played, you wouldn't fancy going back to them. They were rough. But that's where you cut your teeth. If you can get a crowd like that behind you, then playing the London Palladium's a doddle!

"I don't think he personally looks back on that time with any great fondness," John continues, "but I think he learned a lot of toughness. He sharpened up his act to a much more professional level."

Another local band that Dominic appeared in was called Andante, from the musical term meaning *moderately slow tempo*.

"Andante was Tony Phillips, John Houston, Damian Given and Dominic," recalls John. "Damian had his own little recording studio at the time. Damian would have written songs and Dominic would have come in and sung demos for him. My abiding memory of the band is of the boys doing *Paperback Writer* with the four-piece harmony and all. They were really, really good and went on, I would say, for most of 1984."

A stillborn spin-off from Andante was a duo comprising Dominic and John Houston. "They played one small gig in a place in town called The Cellar Bar," says John, "and it wasn't

Dominic's bag at all. He didn't like it and he still can't get his head around it. That gig made him decide, 'Right, I want to do this thing on my own.'"

Four years before he signed with Ritz, Dominic self-financed the recording of his first single, a cover of the Oakridge Boys' country song *Alice In Wonderland* which was subsequently released on the Homespun label and later by Belfast-based Outlet Records.

Interviewed by a local newspaper at the time, Dominic quipped, "The funny thing is I've never once read the *Alice In Wonderland* story. But then the song is only vaguely connected with Lewis Carroll's classic yarn anyway. I just hope it has a fairy tale ending for me."

"He was very, very proud of that single," recalls Louise. "I remember he came home with it and signed it for me. I can't remember the exact wording but it was something like, 'Hopefully there'll be many more.'"

"I remember it well, because it's the only record I'm on!" Exclaims Dominic's younger brother. "I'm on it on backing vocals."

Produced by Mike Morris, the single and its B-side, *You're Always The One,* found Dominic in good voice, although the slow pace and reflective nature of both songs were perhaps an overly demanding choice for an inexperienced recording artist. As a result Dominic's performance understandably lacks the verve, confidence and bite that he would display by the time he recorded for Ritz.

John Kirwan maintains that the released version of *Alice In Wonderland* lacks the sonic power of the original recording.

"*Alice In Wonderland* started off with really big, fat drums and nice keyboard. We came up this Saturday on the way to a gig and Mike Morris was sort of distraught at himself because he'd lost all the punch of it. I don't know if he pressed the wrong button or whatever, but it's not what it should be."

For the first seven years of the 80s, Dominic balanced his musical career with a full time job, even though he confessed in an early interview that he hated getting up in the mornings and described himself as "a night person."

"I would have always known that he wanted to be a singer," recalls his first boss, Declan O'Neill. "It didn't really interfere with his work. As a matter of fact, I would have encouraged him. In later years he would have branched out a little bit and taken on gigs in the south of Ireland and I used to give him time off to go."

As a salesman, Declan describes Dominic as, "Very good. nd me and it was always taking me away from that. So I was in and out all the time, but doing the best with what I could do."

Looking back on the effect of his career on his relationship with his children Dominic says, "I suppose Lee must have been nine or ten when I got my record contract. Colm would have been six or seven and Barry was only three or four. So, really, my family has grown up with me in the music industry. It's not something they don't know about. They know everything about it -how we all lived. They've seen their lifestyle change with it and, in all fairness to them, they've had more comfortable surroundings than I would have had as a kid."

Dominic and Louise's first real marital home was a rented three-bedroom house at 3 Glenelly Gardens.

"It was in an area called Strathroy which, from where we lived, would have been maybe two miles away," says Louise. "It was a completely different area, which we didn't like at all -I think just because it was a different area of the town. It was so totally different. And, at that stage, I actually worked in our end of town."

At least, having the privacy of their own home was an improvement on staying with relatives.

"I think you feel like you're over crowding the place," says Louise of the months she and Dominic lived with her sister

Valerie and her husband Brendan. "We felt at the time it was better than moving in with one of our mums. At least we'd have someone of our own age group and they'd be more understanding. As well as that, Valerie and Brendan own a furniture shop in the town, so they were out all day, really, and you had the house to yourself nearly all day. But when the baby cried, you'd still feel like, 'Oh, my God. We're in the way here.'"

When The Melody Boys eventually went their separate ways, giving in to the need to raise families and earn livings, Barry Bradley, who had served an apprenticeship as an engineer, moved to London in search of gainful employment. He lives there to this day and in the evenings fronts his own band The Breeze. Looking back on his first band with Dominic, he says, "I remember playing Donegal the night before I left. But we had so many good times. The band kinda went from being a pub band to touring Ireland. That was really exciting for youngsters like ourselves. We had some good times along the way."

Good times that Dominic was far from ready to give up. With the demise of The Melody Boys, he continued to front a number of bands, including a short stint with a 50s style rock'n'roll outfit called Hi-De-Hi."

As well as his professional work, Dominic was a regular entrant of talent competitions large and small.

"I know some people call that the kiss of death," he reflected in an interview many years later, "but it worked for me. I won a minor recording contract."

Several years before that, one of the first major talent competitions Dominic entered saw him singing on Ulster Television in the Benson & Hedges Entertainer Of The Year Competition.

"It was run in heats in certain parts of the country," says Dominic. "I remember I won my heat in a place called The

Everglades Hotel in Derry, then I went on to the final in Belfast. There was a panel of judges from within the industry and it was a fella called Pat Woods who actually won. I remember I sang *American Trilogy*."

Naturally, Dominic's family were glued to the television when he made his appearance.

"It was broadcast on St Patrick's Day, 1982, at 9'oclock at night," recalls John. "Derek Batey was the compere. I remember putting a tape recorder up to the TV to record it. Dominic was wearing a big velvet suit, a dicky bow and all. But he sung *American Trilogy* and he did a very good version."

Although he didn't win, Dominic recalls, "It was fun to do. It was a good experience." Dominic also auditioned unsuccessfully for the RTE talent show *Screen Test* and even wrote to the most famous TV talent show of them all, *Opportunity Knocks,* after seeing an advertisement in the *Belfast Telegraph*, although he was never invited to appear on the programme.

Immediately before the many smaller, local competitions that he entered, Dominic says, "I would be calm, cool and collected, but at the same time feeling I was capable. A band would always be supplied and I would do things like *Sweet Caroline* from Neil Diamond. Songs that were audience participation and would show my voice reasonably well. I always maintained that the song *Noreen Bawn* was the winning song for me."

As for losing. . . "I was OK, because from the earliest days as an Irish dancer I was capable of handling disappointment."

"I remember seeing him beaten by people who couldn't wipe the floor," says John. "Adjudicators are strange people. They make strange decisions. But it didn't matter what you threw at him. He got a lot of knocks. But the one constant was that he kept going."

The most important competition Dominic won was organised by pirate radio station Big M, across the border in

Monaghan, in 1988. The prize included a holiday in Portugal and, more importantly, the opportunity to record his first album, *The Green Fields Of Ireland,* which was released on the Music Box label.

Interviewed by the *Ulster Herald* at the time, Dominic says, "There wereupwards of 200 entrants in the competition originally and, when I was announced as the overall winner from the final nine contestants, I just couldn't believe it. This was something I had been aiming at for years and obviously I was over the moon that it had come at last."

Was Louise in the audience the night he won?

"It was an audience vote, so we had to be there!" And did she think he would win?

"I did. Although you never know with these talent competitions. You had to be prepared to lose, even though you may have felt you'd beaten the others on the night, because when the vote came up at the end it mightn't be you."

Asked about his plans for his first album, the *Ulster Herald* quoted Dominic as saying: "I've still to decide what material is going to be on it. Of course, it will be aimed at the Irish market, so there will be nothing to threaten those on *Top Of The Pops.*"

Dominic was, however, beginning to taste life as a pop star. On June 5, 1988, while he was making *The Green Fields Of Ireland* at a studio in Castleblaney, the *Sunday News* ran a large article on the moustached singer under the headline:

Why mob-mania suits star Dominic.

'If you see Dominic Kirwan around town these days it's a fair bet that he will have a smile on his face,' wrote reporter Ian Starrett. *'Because most places the big Omagh guy sings these nights he gets mobbed by beautiful women.*

'Their passion for the Omagh warbler even cost him a pretty penny the other day. Recently he purchased a specially made £200 white stage suit from a London tailor. Then the other night women fans started mobbing their idol and accidentally tore off one of the sleeves.

"'I didn't think local singers got mobbed these days but I'm not complaining mind you. I'm loving every minute of it," said the singer.'

In every respect, *The Green Fields Of Ireland* showed a massive improvement in the singer who had cut *Alice In Wonderland* three years before. Apart from a couple of country songs such as *Paper Roses* and the lilting opener *Candlelight In Wine*, the repertoire was firmly geared to the Irish market with such selections as *My Irish Rose, Roads Of Kildare, Home To Cavan* and *Danny Boy*.

Dominic handled the material with assurance, and offered a particularly fine performance on the strongly written, medium paced title track which, amid a typically sentimental view of rural Ireland, proclaimed a hope for peace at the end of the Troubles.

The highlight of the album, however, was the closing dramatic reading of the traditional ballad *Noreen Bawn* which, to this day, remains one of the most demanded and admired parts of Dominic's repertoire. The production and arrangement of the song would be improved on a later recording for Ritz, but the sheer, raw power of Dominic's impassioned performance on his first album was as striking as anything he would ever record.

Even while Dominic was recording *The Green Fields Of Ireland* there was a buzz that the singer was about to become a major star. Some reports had him about to record a second album for Belfast label Splash Records. In fact, he was about to do a deal with the most successful independent label ever to emerge from England and Ireland, and all the work and struggle he had invested in his music for the past decade was about to pay off. ■

CHAPTER FIVE

Putting on the Ritz

" I WAS the next male recording artist brought on to the label after Daniel O'Donnell," says Dominic, "He was becoming successful -and we were all hearing about this Ritz record label."

For all the power and influence wielded by the major record companies with their colossal promotional budgets, great swathes of music history have been written by independent operators: the little guy with the big idea and an eye for the main chance. In America in the 1950s it was Sam Phillips and his tiny Sun Records label who ushered in the rock'n'roll era by recording the genre's giants Elvis Presley, Carl Perkins, Jerry Lee Lewis and many others. On the other side of the pond thirty-five years later, it was Mick Clerkin's Ritz Records that confounded the majors by mining a huge, neglected market and striking pure gold with a far quieter but in its own way just as controversial form of music -country'n'Irish.

Long before he became one of the world's most successful sellers of records, Michael Clerkin, a quietly spoken, heavy set Irishman, was selling washing machines in his native County Cavan. One of his co-workers was Sean Reilly, a trusted friend whom he would appoint many years later as Daniel

O'Donnell's manager. Moving to England in 1956, when he was sixteen years old, Clerkin worked in pubs and as a sales rep for Initial Towel Supply, before moving into the music business as a roadie and bus driver to Larry Cunningham and The Mighty Avons, who hailed from his home county.

When Cunningham went solo, Clerkin became his manager. He then set up his own record company, Release Records in Ireland, which led him to establish Ritz in London.

" I had caught a song when I was in Nashville, I think it was in 1979, called *One Day At A Time*, which was written by Marijohn Wilkin," says Clerkin at his current base in Dublin. "We recorded it with a girl called Gloria and it was Number One for weeks and weeks in Ireland. I went over to the UK to try and get a release on it. I went to four or five of the major record companies and they all said, 'No, it's never going to happen in this country.'"

By the late autumn of 1979, however, *One Day At A Time* was at the top of the UK charts. The record was all over the airwaves and eventually became a million seller.

"Unfortunately it wasn't with Gloria, it was Lena Martell. The last company that I went to had Lena Martell on the label and they had that track on an album. They just got it out there and away it went. It annoyed me to say the least. So I said, 'I'm going to go over there and have a go at doing it myself."

The name Ritz Records was coined by an Italian, Roberto Danovo. In 1981, Clerkin had travelled to London and begun working with his long time friend Peter Dempsey, who was a successful Irish manager. The two made their base at Ryan's Hotel near Kings Cross before joining forces with record producer Danovo, who had just set up Ritz.

"I was looking for a label with a classy name and Ritz was ideal," remembers Clerkin.

The label's first single was by Irishman Joe Dolan, who had enjoyed a run of UK chart hits some years before, beginning with *Make Me An Island* in 1969. The second single was by a band called Sheeba, a Eurovision Song Contest entrant managed by Dempsey. However, it was Ritz's third signing, the Fureys And Davey Arthur that put Ritz on the map, with the label's first hit in October 1981.

"I was approached by Jim Hand who managed the Fureys," says Clerkin. "He said, 'Would I be interested in releasing *When You Were Sweet Sixteen* in the UK?' I said, 'OK.' I took it to Terry Wogan, who I'd known from years before he even went to the UK. That was the difference between then and now. You wouldn't get that situation now. It ended up being a top twenty single. They appeared on *Top Of The Pops* and the album sold about a 120,000 or 130,000 copies.

"The next one was Foster & Allen. Again, the management, who were based here in Ireland, asked if I'd be interested in releasing *A Bunch Of Thyme*. They'd been turned down twice in the UK, then they went with a company that ended up going bust. I said, 'Yeah, I'll take it on. We'll have a go.' And again Radio Two were very good to us."

A Bunch Of Thyme also made the UK Top 20 and was followed by a string of chart entries for Foster & Allen that stretched into the mid-80s, including the now classic country'n'Irish numbers, *Maggie* and *I Will Love You All My Life.*

In early 1982, Clerkin took over Ritz, buying out Danovo who felt that the label was no longer going in the direction he had originally intended. Peter Dempsey died and Clerkin recruited former CBS and RCA promotions man Eamon Leahy as a partner to run Ritz's concert division. Mick's daughter Anne joined the team as company secretary and general manager, and former EMI man Paddy McIntyre was headhunted by Mick to handle Ritz's relations with regional radio.

McIntyre, incidentally, may never live down his reputation in Ritz folklore as the man who put the phone down on Elvis. It was an easy mistake to make. "Uh, this is Elvis Presley," said an

American voice on the phone one day at McIntyre's previous job. "Of course you are," said Paddy, suspecting a wind-up, and replaced the receiver. A few moments later his boss came in and said, "I'm expecting a call from Elvis. Make sure you put him through…"

The other favourite story about McIntyre is that when he left EMI to join Ritz, his former boss Kay O'Dwyer, told him, "You're mad to go with those Irish guys -they'll last about six months." Of course, whenever Clerkin met O'Dwyer after that, he couldn't resist quipping, "It's sixteen years now, and he's still here!"

After months of working out of first a hotel, then a flat in North London, Ritz finally moved into proper offices in Covent Garden and then to new premises in Kilburn, close to London's most famous Irish dance hall, the Galtymore, where the company was based when Dominic joined them.

By that time the Ritz roster had grown to include a mild mannered singer from Donegal called Daniel O'Donnell. The younger brother of established Irish entertainer Margo O'Donnell, Daniel had been broke and on the verge of quitting the music business when he was discovered by Clerkin and signed to Ritz in 1985. He began to blossom into the biggest easy listening star ever to emerge from Ireland, selling out concerts across the UK and developing an obsessive following among his predominantly mature, female audience. Daniel's third Ritz album, *Don't Forget To Remember* entered the UK country charts at Number One and his 1988 release *From The Heart* crossed over on to the pop charts amid a television advertising campaign that was arranged through a licensing deal with Telstar.

From the inception of Ritz, Mick Clerkin believed that there was a large slice of the British market place whose taste in tuneful, easy listening music was not being met by the mainstream record labels. More than any of the artists he had dealt with up to that point, the success of Daniel O'Donnell, who was fast becoming a media phenomenon, appeared to prove Clerkin right on a massive scale.

O'Donnell's success also seemed to pave the way forward for another Irish singer with a strong appeal to the female audience, Dominic Kirwan. Daniel and Dominic were very different performers. But they sang a similar blend of American country music, Irish songs and covers of pop songs from the 60s and 70s. The chief difference, at a glance, was that Dominic was the more dynamic showman, with an inherently bigger voice and a raunchier sex appeal. That, at least, was the view of Dominic's former manager from the Knock-na-Moe Castle Hotel days, Charlie McBrien, who re-surfaced in Dominic's life to broker the deal between Dominic and his old pal Mick Clerkin.

"Charlie had managed me for about a year or so in the early 80s, but nothing materialised and we went our separate ways," says Dominic. "I kept working for the next five or six years and there was an interest that started to be created in the North West region of Northern Ireland. A little bit of a buzz was happening. Charlie knew about me, so it was him that actually contacted me and talked about getting together and letting bygones be bygones, because we did have a slight falling out back in the early days. Charlie then introduced me to Mick Clerkin."

"Charlie and I had worked together in the 60s when I first got into the business," recalls Clerkin. "I was a road manager with Larry Cunningham & The Mighty Avons who were big in the show band days and Charlie was the manager of that band at the time. I left the band scene about 1968 and we met up some years later. We didn't have much contact in the meantime. So, Charlie asked me to have a look at Dominic with a view to recording him. Which I duly did."

"I also think there might have been a bit of information filtered through to Mick from Daniel O'Donnell," says Dominic. " Daniel was very aware of what was going on at that time around the countryside. I didn't know Daniel personally, but I had met him and he had been hearing about me through the little media attention I was picking up in Ireland.

"I remember going to see Daniel at the local St Enda's GAA club in Omagh," Dominic continues. "Somebody must have told him I was there. He said he'd meet me after the show and I remember sitting with him in the car afterwards, the two of us. He was basically telling me what was happening to him. Things were on the up for him. But not only was he telling me that, he was also asking me about my career. Not long after that, I was approached by Ritz, so I think Daniel may have hinted to Mick Clerkin that he should listen to me. That may have started the ball rolling."

Speaking at his office in Dublin, Clerkin confirms that Daniel had indeed mentioned Dominic to him.

"More than once in fact." says the Ritz boss. "Maybe half a dozen times. Daniel would have mentioned his name and suggested that I go and see him and it was probably because of the prompting from Charlie that I did go and see him.

"Daniel had a big influence on Dominic getting involved with Ritz," Clerkin elaborates, "because he believed that he was very, very good, and Daniel was someone who would push artists or recommend them if he thought they had potential. He's never been one to think, 'He might be competition one day.' That's not the nature of the guy. So Daniel would have said, 'Dominic is a bit different to me. He's more rock'n'roll,' and that he would be good for Ritz. I remember he did have quite a lot of belief in him. Charlie McBrien was also pushing the Dominic cause, so I had him thrown at me from two fronts."

Daniel advised Dominic to listen to the people around him. "To try and determine which are the right moves and the wrong moves. He's more interested in seeing things going well for you. On his last tour, my album *Stone In Love With You* was played at the beginning of the show, in the interval and at the very end. If I was told that once, I was told that 101 times. So, that's the type of guy he is."

As for any rivalry between the artists, dreamed up by some fans and media commentators, Dominic says, "Never. We've never been rivals. Definitely not with me and I would say most of all not with him. I respect Daniel. I think he does an amazing job. I think he handles the media attention very well. But, as for rivalry, absolutely not. We are two very different acts."

Spurred on by Daniel and Charlie, Clerkin went to see Dominic perform at Frankie's Nite Club in County Donegal.

"Frankie had once a year what he called a free dance, where he gave the patrons around the region a night out and he supplied the band. We got the opportunity to play at it. There was a very, very large crowd and Mick Clerkin came along with Charlie."

"My first impression was a young Tony Christie," says Clerkin, drawing a comparison with a singer who had a big UK hit in 1971 with *I Did What I Did For Maria*.

"I think that would be the best way to describe him. More Tony Christie than Tom Jones. I did see Christie some years back in Dublin and, I think, in England as well. So that was my first impression, basically. He did quite a lot of Irish songs in his set as well."

Dominic got a message telling him to stop at Charlie's house on the way past from the show. "I stopped at his home at maybe four o'clock in the morning. We got talking over a cup of tea. Mick then said that he liked what he heard and that he would be interested in recording me and would I be interested? That was more or less the start of it all. I remember very well that being the 7th of January, 1989."

Clerkin never filled the young hopeful's head with big plans for the future, "Never. At the end of the day, they're a record company. They're not a management company, you know? I think a lot of people at the beginning thought they were a management company. But they weren't. So, as for plans, it was all about recording and getting out there and getting on with sales," said Dominic.

Recorded within a month or two of his first meeting with Clerkin, Dominic's first release on Ritz was a single called *The Green Hills Are Rolling Still*, a song written by another soon-to-be star of the label, Liverpool school teacher Charlie Landsborough. The song and its B-side, *Golden Dreams*, which Dominic had already cut on his album, *The Green Fields Of Ireland*, also appeared on an EP which was completed by the tracks *More Than Yesterday* and *The Little Cabin On The Hill*.

Shortly afterwards, Dominic released his first Ritz album, *Try A Little Kindness*. The producer of all the recordings was Shaun 'Mudd' Wallace who recorded the singer at his own Homestead Studio in Randelstown, about 50 miles north east of Omagh, near Antrim.

Of the decision to use Wallace, Clerkin says, "It was convenience more than anything else. I'd heard some good reports about Shaun as a musician, really. They were both in the same part of the world, making it convenient to do it there. Dominic was doing quite a bit of work, and trying to record and work at the same time is not easy."

"My first impression of Dominic was that he was a good singer!" says Wallace, who, after a period of ill health, is still recording at Homestead. "He had a very good voice. He was quite young at that time and he had a mature voice for his age. At the beginning he was probably nervous, like anybody else. But I don't think he was ever really shy of recording. He took to it like a duck to water.

"Even later on, he was always open to criticism and taking direction in the studio," Wallace continues. "We've taken ages when we've had to, just to get it right. He was always prepared to stay in the studio late and do a bit of extra work to get a vocal right. Some people would come in and go, 'Right, there's the vocal. That's all you're getting. That's all I'm prepared to do.' But Dominic was OK that way. He was prepared to work."

"Shaun was a great character to work with," says Dominic.

"He's a very intelligent guy. Very technically minded.

"He's also a diabetic. I remember him having to take his top ups of Lucozade, and eating his digestive biscuits. Those are the things I remember. But it was my first major producer, I suppose, and it was all new to me. I was just totally in awe of the whole recording industry. It's very difficult to remember all the different situations."

In contrast to the predominantly Irish content of Dominic's debut album, *Try A Little Kindness* almost entirely comprised familiar American country songs, such as *Oh! Lonesome Me, Careless Hands, Sea Of Heartbreak* and *Before The Next Teardrop Falls*.

Vocally, it was one of the best country albums of the year. Dominic had taken further strides forward in terms of confidence and presence since *The Green Fields Of Ireland*. His readings were utterly assured, there was an effortless elasticity in his voice and he wrapped the lyrics in warmth and feeling, whether it was a slow, velvety ballad like *I'll Leave This World Loving You* or the foot tapping *Achin' Breaking Heart*.

The chief difference between English and Irish interpretations of American country music over the years is that the English have often fallen into the trap of adopting obviously unauthentic American accents while the Irish have been happier to be themselves and create their own brand of country'n'Irish music. Dominic epitomised this difference by sounding as natural on purely American songs such as *Careless Hands* as he did on the more obviously Irish sounding tracks like *More Than Yesterday* (which, incidentally, featured the accordion playing of his later musical director Jim McVeigh although, at the time of the recording, the two men never met).

Perhaps because of their roots in the dance hall tradition, Irish musicians have also traditionally outclassed their English counterparts when it comes to romantic country ballads or gently swinging up tempo songs. With exactly the right amount of dripping piano notes, slick strings and ringing steel guitar, the musical setting that Wallace created for Dominic combined with the singer's faultless performances created an album of pure class.

The only thing 'wrong' with *Try A Little Kindness* was that, fresh and enjoyable as Dominic's interpretations were, most of the songs he tackled had long been done to death by other performers. The arrangements, like the songs, similarly reflected the middle of the road, pop-leaning output of Nashville in the 70s and even the 60s and 50s, rather than the New Country that was enjoying a sales boom across the Atlantic in the late 80s and even beginning to gain credibility with a young audience in the UK.

Such an unashamedly old-fashioned approach was undoubtedly well targeted at the older, nostalgia orientated market with which Ritz had been enjoying such immense success with Daniel O'Donnell, but was unlikely to alert critics or DJs to the arrival of a vital new musical force.

For his own part, Dominic claims the sound of his first Ritz album was not representative of his stage show at the time. Indeed, he goes so far as to say, "I would say that it wasn't what I wanted to do, now that I look back on it. I maybe wanted to do some of the songs. But I felt it was more musician orientated than artist focused. It was a mixture of the producer and the musicians he wanted to use getting more out of it for their playing purposes than I personally wanted for myself."

Perhaps confirming a degree of the self interest that Dominic hints at, Wallace says, "It was quite a big album for me at the time. It was the first time I had worked with Ritz on a bigger budget album. I remember doing a lot of work, hoping to impress them."

Of the decision to cut such frequently recorded material as *Careless Hands* and *Heartaches By The Number,* Dominic says, "Some of the material would have been stuff we were doing on the road and other selections would have come through the record company. I was probably playing very much the safe game at the time because I was an unknown artist then. So, for me going out on the road it was important for people to at least know the songs."

Was Mick Clerkin involved with the song selection process?

"Well, Mick always is," says Wallace. "That's his big thing in Ritz. He was always picking material. He seemed to have a very good ear for a song that was going to do well. It probably comes from his involvement in the show band days. A good ear for what went well on the dance floor. I remember with most of the Ritz albums, if it was a 14 song album, they would have already picked out 20 songs and we would have recorded 20 songs. Then, whatever ones recorded best usually ended up being the ones we used. Occasionally we went back to the others and you could use them on something else."

Asked if he had strong ideas about the material that he would like his artists to record, Clerkin says, "Not necessarily. We more or less agreed on that, I would think, in most cases. We'd sit down and go through 25 songs or whatever. We'd narrow it down and come up with the eventual 14."

Surprisingly, Clerkin claims his own formative tastes in music were not as deeply rooted in traditional country music and Irish music as one might suppose from the records Ritz has released over the years.

"A guy came to see me one time from Irish radio," says Clerkin. "He had a programme on late at night and he had a feature on that programme, once a week, where he featured the music of people who were in the business. He wouldn't have you in the studio or anything. He would just meet you and ask you what your favourite three songs were when you were growing up.

"I remember I had him doing a voice over for me one day on some commercial and he said, 'Oh, I must do my three selections with you some time. You might want to let me know up front because I've probably got fewer country songs and I might have to try and find them.' I said, 'Well, I don't think you'll have too much of a problem.' My early favourites were Bing Crosby, Nat King Cole and people like that. I never heard too much country music in the earlier days. That surprised him. It was people like Frank Sinatra and Dean Martin."

A rare original song on *Try A Little Kindness* was another Charlie Landsborough composition, *Heaven Knows*. Beginning with the words "If people dressed in colours according to their deeds then many leading men would dress in black..." the song was a typically gentle and poetic Landsborough composition which cleverly combined folksy philosophy with yearning love song in an appealingly sentimental confection.

"We listened to a few Landsborough songs," says Wallace. "Charlie hadn't been signed to Ritz at that time and his publisher was bombarding me with his material to try and get artists that I was recording to cover them. I think at that time Ritz were basically just looking out for songs that were unique to Dominic. New songs to him. That was the type of thing we were listening to."

Referring to the velvety closer *St Theresa Of The Roses* and the sprightly *Golden Dreams* which Dominic reprised from *The Green Fields Of Ireland,* Wallace adds, "Dominic had picked out a few things that he had been doing in his live set as well. Some of the more up-tempo, Irish type things."

Clerkin explains why Dominic recorded tried and trusted material. "Ideally, it would be nice to be doing original songs. But it's very difficult to come across strong enough original material. If you're a successful songwriter and you get the opportunity of going to Westlife with your song or Dominic Kirwan, where are you gonna go? That's the problem. The big acts tend to get the big songs."

"*Heaven Knows* was really good for the register of Dominic's voice," says Wallace. "He's got a powerful voice when he sings in the higher register.

"We messed about with quite a few key changes to find what would suit his voice best," the producer continues. "I usually found with Dominic, the higher I could push the key of the song the better it works for him. He's got a more powerful voice when he's belting out the high notes."

Intriguingly, the sleeve notes to *Try A Little Kindness* credit Dominic as producer and his road band as musicians on four songs, including the title track. Dominic denies, however, that he has ever had any aspirations to occupy the producer's chair.

"I've always looked back at that..." The singer begins with a thoughtful frown, before saying, "I personally believed that at the time there were certain tracks that Mudd didn't want to get involved in and, rather than put his name on them he just put our names to it. As for production, there was very little production to them. I never really thought a lot about it. I thought that was something he doesn't want to be credited for, so we got the credit for it. But it's no big deal."

"On those four songs he brought his own band in," says Wallace. "They were basically done as live tracks in the studio, so I didn't have much of an input as producer. Those particular songs were added to the album afterwards, just to add a bit more of a flavour of what was going on with the live band. A bit more of a reference to what was going on in the concerts."

With product to sell, Ritz's priority was to get Dominic seen by the largest audience possible. To that end, they booked him as support to label mate and fellow County Tyrone resident Philomena Begley and her special guest Mick Flavin on a 13 date tour of England and Scotland beginning at the Forum in Hatfield on September 24, 1989.

"Philly was a real big artist in the industry as far as I was concerned," says Dominic. "She was the Queen of Country Music. She pulled in the big crowds. I would have danced to her band the Rambling Men. But I would have never known her personally. I've always been more than grateful for that fortnight, because not only was she great as an artist to watch, but she was fun to be with. I've always admired how she handled herself in many situations. So it's ironic that I'd always known her and seen her many times and that the first tour I did was with her."

The following year, Dominic undertook a five week UK tour as support to black American country star Charley Pride and, in 1991, he opened an even longer tour for country legend Tammy Wynette. It was all part of a plan to create a demand for Dominic so that he could tour the same large theatres in his own right.

"Lots of artists have ideas that they want to be big stars and stars of television and all that, but it's not as glamorous as that," says Mick Clerkin, whose label was one of the few record companies to have its own in-house concert division to promote its artists on the road.

"There's a lot of work," continues Clerkin, "which Dominic has always put into it, like Daniel has. They are both real professionals and would take on whatever workload was necessary to promote, in terms of travelling to radio stations and doing TV work. In Dominic's case, his biggest break was probably touring the UK as support to Charley Pride. I knew the promoter, Robert Pratt, and I asked him, 'Would there be a chance of getting Dominic on there? And it worked well in terms of getting Dominic across to a broader audience in the UK. The Tammy Wynette tour would have enhanced the thing even further.

"Unfortunately," adds Clerkin, "those tours are not easy to get any more for new artists coming along. Tammy Wynette is no longer with us, Charley Pride isn't touring that much and there's nobody else really. That was the platform for launching new acts, if you like."

How did Dominic find the transition from club and function work to playing concerts in large theatres?

"I found it difficult and I probably still have difficulties with it," admits the singer. "although I prefer theatre work the best. My first opportunity to get on that level was when I toured with Philomena Begley and I knew then that that's what I wanted to do: people coming to the theatre and sitting down and watching. No alcohol involved. Non-smoking atmosphere.

"For the performer, it's a harder thing, mentally. It's about getting out there and creating that rapport with the audience. Being sensible in what you do and say. Just generally getting that entertainment value over. It's a more conscious thing, whereas in the cabaret, club and dance situation -of course you don't want to let yourself down -but there's a little bit of flippancy and throwaway there that you wouldn't get away with in a theatre."

"I believe 100% in presentation. When I look back, I sometimes think, 'Good lord, did I wear that?' But you go through different stages. People have got to look at you and know you're not necessarily coming on to the stage wearing exactly what people are wearing on the streets. I think that's part of the respect you give your audience."

When Ritz eventually stopped booking their acts on the road, Stewart Laurie's Pinetree Promotions took over Dominic's tours on the mainland. Laurie had, however, been involved in co-promoting Dominic's Scottish shows from the early 90s. He also worked with O'Donnell, Landsborough and Mary Duff. But, he recalls, "Dominic would have been the one out of all of them that people over here wanted. He had good looks. He had sex appeal. He was a good singer. He had a good band.

"Dominic's a class performer suitable for the stage," Laurie continues in his deep Scottish drawl. "That's the difference between Dominic and a lot of the Irish artists -and one they can't see. In Ireland you're playing in a dance hall environment. You'll get a good crowd on a Saturday night, a good crowd on Friday and maybe a good crowd on Sunday. But in the concert environment over here they haven't got the appeal that Dominic's got. They haven't got the ability to get across to people and be a good ambassador and create a rapport with the audience. Dominic Kirwan has got that and that's why he's successful over here. He's a concert artist. He's not a dance hall artist."

Dominic could, however, shine in either environment.

"There's always this resentment among the Irish artists about what the other acts are doing," Laurie continues. "People would resent Dominic for the crowds he draws over here and say, 'We get bigger crowds than him in Ireland.' But they're talking about a Saturday night dance. The fact is, Dominic could play a Saturday night dance and add maybe 500 to the usual audience. Joe Dolan would do the same. Because they were regarded by a lot of people, even in Ireland, as being superior."

Finally, Laurie identifies another aspect of Dominic's appeal that has ensured his success in the UK.

"In this type of music. . ." Laurie takes a deep breath. "This sounds a hard thing to say, and a lot of people might not agree with me, because they'll say, 'I'm not like that,' although a lot of them are. . . But a lot of lonely people go to these shows. A lot of people who live on their own. Mothers whose families have gone away and this sort of thing. There's a loneliness. They like to identify with something, so they identify themselves with the likes of Dominic Kirwan. They put the photographs up in the house. They play his videos and he's sort of, 'This is the guy I can turn to. The guy I can talk to. The guy I can think about.'

"When they go to the shows they want to meet him in the autograph queue and maybe tell him their personal things, and he stands there and listens to all that. And, all due credit to him, he handles it very well.

"What I'm trying to emphasis is that in this business we are catering for lonely people. People that need reassurance. People that need somebody to identify with. Dominic fits that bill perfectly. He's a good, clean, family entertainer." ■

CHAPTER SIX

Ghost of a Chance

FOR HIS second Ritz album, *Love Without End*, Dominic headed south to Dublin where he recorded under the helmsmanship of Eamon Campbell, who was a member of long-standing Irish group, The Dubliners.

"It was a different producer, different thoughts, different ideas, different sounds," says Dominic. "There were a lot of older things on there, but some newer things as well."

"I'd worked with Daniel O'Donnell for Ritz," says Campbell, "and Mick Clerkin had been a very good friend for years. He told me he was discovering this good singer called Dominic Kirwan and he asked me to produce an album."

"I'd worked with Eamon on other projects at the time," reveals Clerkin. "Eamon initially was a session guitar player and banjo player. I knew him from back when he was playing in a club with Dermot O'Brien. He had produced successful albums on Foster & Allen. In fact, I think he produced half a dozen Foster & Allen albums, and some of the hits as well, like the Landsborough-written *I Will Love You All My Life*. I thought Eamon would be a good choice for Dominic."

"I think Mick wanted to break him into the same market as, say, Daniel and Foster & Allen," says Campbell. "He thought that the songs   we picked, and the treatment, would get across not just to country fans. If you go pure country, you're gonna lose listeners. There are many people out there who don't like certain types of country music. So it was more middle of the road."

That said, *Love Without End* was undeniably country. It simply represented the more sophisticated, pop-leaning sounds to have come out of Nashville over the years, whether the classic, string-laden Nashville sounds of the late 60s and early 70s that Campbell adopted for the much recorded ballad *Almost Persuaded*, or the leaner, lyrical well-crafted country that the more traditional of Nashville's modern stars, such as George Strait, were recording at the dawn of the Nineties.

Looking back, ten years later, from the verge of making his third album in Nashville, Dominic says, "What I'm doing today was probably done in Dublin in 91, 92 – only, I suppose, with an Irish flavour to it. To some extent I think we were probably a little ahead of our time."

Campbell invited Dominic to his home.

"When I was producing, I would   get the artist to come to my house. We'd have a chat and just try to get to know the people, so you're not meeting them for the first time in the studio. We had a list of songs which we whittled down, and I had a guitar there, and we kinda ran through them. Picked keys and discussed arrangements. So, before I went into the studio with Dominic, I would say I knew him. We had become very friendly."

The sessions were recorded at Dublin's Windmill Lane Studios. "There was a lovely atmosphere about the place. And it was totally isolated, even though you were in the heart of Dublin. When you closed the door that was it. The world just ceased, outside.

"There's a team of players I always used," Campbell continues, "Des Moore on guitar, John Drummond on bass. . .

I had an understanding with them whereby they'd come in and if it was going well there was no such thing as three hours, the old union laws and all that shit, taking breaks and so on. If it was going well we'd keep going."

"Dominic was so easy to work with," says Campbell, "and I have to say this -this is not bullshitting -he's a great singer!

"He just stands there and sings. Occasionally, maybe he hasn't taken enough breath, or there's a little mispronunciation and sometimes little things like that you'd drop in. You wanted it to be right and, of course, with new technology, you can edit one word. But I'd say 99% of the songs were two run-throughs and then a take."

It was the start of a lasting friendship.

"I'd joined The Dubliners by then. I'm still with them," Campbell reminisces. "I remember we were doing a gig outside Donegal town and Dominic and Louise arrived. Jeez! We were up to seven the next morning. Big sing song!"

Dominic felt even more comfortable working with Eamon that he did with Shaun Wallace.

Comparing his experiences of working with Dominic and O'Donnell, Campbell says: "Their personalities were actually quite alike. But Daniel would be more reserved. Dominic would come out for a pint with you and a bit of a laugh and a *craic*. That wouldn't be Daniel's scene."

Far more sophisticated than *Try A Little Kindness*, in terms of material and arrangement, *Love Without End* opened with *Like Father, Like Son*, a powerful, contemporary country song from the pens of top Nashville tunesmiths Paul Overstreet and Don Schlitz. Dominic delivered the easy paced lyric with an assurance and presence that would have given the finest American country stars pause for thought. In fact, viewed in retrospect, Dominic's performance leaves the listener to wonder how many millions of albums he would have sold had he been born in Texas and signed to a major Nashville label.

"That was a hell of a song! It would have been a fairly new song at the time. Mick used to get a lot of newly written songs from Nashville. Some of them wouldn't have been done before. They'd just be demos," says Campbell.

"What I loved doing was getting the brand new songs with Dominic because he was great at taking direction. You'd suggest something and he knew straight away what you were after. There was a song on the second album we did called *Absent Friends* and if you heard the demo and then you hear his version you'd never believe it was the same song.

"That's the thing with new songs. It's like an artist painting a picture. You have the bones and then you can dress it up. Try and make it better."

As for the reason so many covers appear on Ritz releases generally, Campbell says, "I think this is also to do with the record buying public. You'll get away with sticking in maybe two or three new ones, but if they don't recognise titles they're very inclined not to buy the album. If it was me, personally, it would all be original stuff. Unfortunately it doesn't sell."

With a knowing chuckle, Campbell concludes: "And they (the record company) are not looking at the artistic quality -they're looking at the money!"

The strongest contemporary Nashville song on the album was the title track, *Love Without End, Amen*, which was a Number One on the American country charts for George Strait in the year that Dominic recorded it.

A perfectly crafted example of a cyclical Nashville song, the lyric dealt with the nature of a father's love being strong enough to forgive the mistakes of a son. In the first verse the singer was a young lad, expecting to be reprimanded by his father for fighting at school. In the second verse, the singer had grown up to be a dad himself, learning how to forgive his own son. In the final verse, the singer dreams of standing outside the Pearly Gates, fully expecting to be turned away for his earthly trespasses, only to discover that the Father, God, is equally forgiving of his sons.

Dominic's rendition   of the lyric left no doubt that he fully identified with the song's message.

"It all comes down to words,"   says   the singer. "I was reading a thing on Elvis last night and it more or less said that although he didn't write many songs himself, he sang a lot of songs about how he looked at life and how he felt about life. Now that I'm reflecting on my life and my career in music, that's what I was doing, too. Songs like *Love Without End* were about father-son relationships and I was able to say what I wanted to say through the words of a song. Lee would have been nine at that stage, Colm would have been seven, Barry would have been about four -and Jonathan was just a twinkle in my eye. Then there was my own relationship with my father who died when I was 17. That was important to me and I think I was able to relate to all those things."

A major part of the appeal of *Love Without End*   were the lush but sympathetic string arrangements that Campbell tailored   to Dominic's performance.

"I always insist on the singer being there and doing a guide vocal," explains the producer. "I'd start off with just the rhythm section and when I'd get the rhythm section done with the guide vocal, I'd go off and start thinking about over dubs. I'd have a chat with Mick, or Dominic, and just tell them how I see things. Then I would get him to sing before I would do any over dubs. Then, if there were strings or vocal backings, I might have the strings do something in keeping with his vocal phrasing, rather than have the whole thing written and have to say, 'You can't sing it that way.'"

"Eamon was very much into vocals," remembers Dominic. "You can hear that in a song like *Almost Persuaded*. It was about clarity and pronunciation.

I was a younger artist at the time and probably a lot cleaner and crisper than I would be, now. There would be a lot more age to the voice, now."

Although most of the music on *Love Without End* was American country music, the finale found Dominic returning to the traditional Irish ballad with which he had closed *The Green Fields Of Ireland*, and which he had been singing since The Melody Boys -*Noreen Bawn*.

"When people jump up and say, 'I remember the first record I bought,' I sometimes think to myself, 'You must have done very little in between,'" says Dominic who, naturally, *can't* remember the first record he ever bought does, however, have a vivid memory of buying the single *Noreen Bawn.*

"I picked that song up when I was about 15, 16 years of age. I went into a record shop in Bridge Street, which is no longer there, and it was actually in the cheap box sitting on the desk. I was looking through them and I remember it was 25p. It was by a guy called D.J. Curtain and I remember thinking, 'What a song! What a ballad!' I'd heard the song many times before, but I'd heard it done in the old waltz way and it meant nothing to me. Maybe with D.J. Curtain it was the voice that caught me first. Then I realised what the song was about. It was about emigration. About people having to go away from the country. That's the sort of background I grew up in and, again, I was able to relate to it. It meant something to me.

"I recorded it first of all on *The Green Fields Of Ireland.* Then we had the chance to do it with the big string section. It was good to get the opportunity to do a good live vocal performance."

Looking back on the song's importance in his career, Dominic adds, "It's the sort of song that would have introduced me into the business. A lot of my earlier days would have been spent in talent competitions and *Noreen Bawn* was a song that I would finish off one section of a performance. I really felt *Noreen Bawn* was one of the clinchers for me, and one of the songs that took me through life."

Another track that seemed at odds with the general tone of the album was the uptempo, happy-go-lucky *Life Is What You Make It*. Although it's not a song that would have followed the likes of *Almost Persuaded* or *Stranger Things Have Happened* on a George Jones or George Strait album, Dominic rightly defends the inclusion of the uplifting, life affirming number.

"It was written by Theresa O'Donnell in Ireland and, if you listen to the words of it, they're really quite straight forward. You might look on it as being a silly song and it really was a throwaway song. But, I didn't do it for many, many years, I started to do it this year and it's going down a storm in the show. So, it goes to show that the words are very important to people. And the words are very strong. It's a very sensible song. They're not stupid, silly words."

Although it didn't receive a fraction of the attention it deserved, *Love Without End* got good airplay for the singer, who was quickly establishing himself as a live draw. Although he was still playing smaller venues such as hotels, social clubs and the smaller theatres and arts centres, there was seemingly not a night when Dominic was not playing to a packed adoring audience somewhere in England, Ireland or Scotland, and the 'sold out' notices were starting to go up everywhere.

As testament to his hectic schedule, Dominic recalls the rush to record his first Ritz video, *Dominic Kirwan Live*, which was released in 1990.

"The big memory of my first video was leaving home about five in the morning, grabbing a flight out of Belfast into Glasgow, getting two taxis from Glasgow airport down to Dundee and arriving about two in the afternoon. I think our flight was delayed. Then we went to the theatre for a sound check, shooting our very first video that night. Then it was pack up again, grab a few hours' sleep, then the first flight out of Glasgow because we were playing back in Ireland."

"It's not the way to prepare for your first video!"

That video, however, was to prove important in his life, not least because it introduced him to his long term friends and sponsors Jim and Kath McLarnon of Stamford Van & Car Hire who, for the last decade, have provided the vehicles that keep his touring show on the road.

"I had a car accident," says Kath McLarnon at her home in Cheshire. "I was laid up for seven months, not walking."

To pass the endless hours of enforced rest, Kath watched Irish music videos brought over by a friend. Her favourite quickly turned out to be by a new singer called Dominic Kirwan.

"As I couldn't move about, I used to have them put Dominic's tape in and just watch it all day long. I loved the way he sang. I loved the way he danced. I loved everything about him."

"I noticed that every time I went in the front room, Dominic's tape was on," smiles Jim, who by that time ran one of Manchester's most successful fleets of hire vehicles. "Down went the knitting. She had to concentrate on him."

In fact, Jim came to believe that the uplifting nature of Dominic's performance was instrumental in his wife's recovery. The first time Kath saw Dominic on the screen, she swore that one day she would see him live. So once Kath was back on her feet following a successful operation, Jim decided to treat his wife by booking Dominic to play at their 30th wedding anniversary party in June, 1991.

"Jim just idolises Kath," says Dominic, "He would do anything for her. So he took it upon himself to make a contact with a friend of his called Pat Jordan, another Irish singer who's based in Manchester, and said, 'Look, is there any way you could make contact with this man? How would you get to him?'

"The contact was made," Dominic continues, "I was approached and I said, 'Well, fair enough, I'm interested, there's no doubt about that.' The only problem was that I didn't have any work in England that particular weekend. I asked Pat to wait and see if I could pick up another couple of shows to make it financially viable for me to go to England for the weekend which I did.

"I arrived at the hotel and we did the function. The next day, we got talking and Jim said he'd be interested in sponsoring me for vehicles and things on the road. That's what happened and they've been part of my life and my career for the last ten years."

"At the time we'd sponsored a bowling competition for years and years," says Jim, "and Kath said, 'Maybe they don't appreciate us as much as we thought. Why don't you drop that and sponsor Dominic?'"

"We've sponsored Pat Jordan and Finnegan's Rainbow, in a small way, for the past 20 years," adds Jim. "We get quite a few coming over here from Ireland trying to earn a shilling and we're always here to help them."

"I wouldn't say Dominic was struggling at the time," says Kath. "He was a busy lad then. But my husband just tried to make it easier for him on the road."

"Not only have they been sponsoring me," says Dominic, "They've made their home my home in England. When I have days off, that's where I go."

McLarnon's sponsorship of Dominic goes far deeper than business. In fact their company name no longer appears on the Shogun 4X4, band mini-bus and Scania equipment lorry they provide for him.

"We did have the name on in the beginning," says Jim, "But it gives Dominic a little bit of privacy. If he goes out for a meal with his family it means he can park up without being hassled. The business side never really came into it. Dominic travels the UK and Ireland. My core business comes out of south Manchester, which Dominic rarely touches. A lot of my customers wouldn't know who he is. So it's nearly always been more friendship than business."

"When I met Dominic, his personality. . . his kindness. . . everything about him was so real so genuine," says Kath. "I love him like a son. Somehow there was a bond there.

"My husband took to Dominic right away." And Jim admits that he sometimes does think of Dominic as the son he never had.

"I get phone calls from him on a regular basis, and my words are, 'What can I do for you, son?'"

"I lost my father when I was 17 and I suppose over the years there have been times when Jim has been a fatherly figure," says Dominic. "I've been able to turn to him for advice, because he's a businessman. They've become dear friends and I've been there through all aspects of their lives. So we've helped each other."

"As two families -Kath and I and Louise and Dominic- we just clicked," says Jim.

Describing himself as "a fate man," Dominic believes his meeting with the McLarnons was "meant to happen." Not least, because he normally wouldn't have taken on a private party in 1991.

"I hadn't done a private function in a long, long time. "The biggest problem was that I didn't know how to price it. I wasn't one to be smart with the man. I didn't want to be over expensive. I wanted to give him value for money and know at least that the show was going to be done for the right reasons. But once I'd made a decision about the price, Jim changed that on me. That's how generous a man he is, and how genuine he is."

Of his decision to take on the private party in the first place, Dominic says, "I thought of Jim's promise to Kath and I thought, 'If I can help this man out I'll help him.' Maybe that's the reason that we clicked. He probably spotted that I did help him."

Two other people joined Dominic's 'family' on the road in

the early 90s: his personal assistant Peter McGlone and his dresser, Ali Connor.

Having first met McGlone, along with Charlie McBrien, at the Knock-na-Moe Castle Hotel in Omagh a decade before, Dominic says, "Peter was the manager of the hotel. We had the vehicles from the company at that time. We'd come back and it would be Peter I would go to meet to hand the money over and take the percentages out of. The usual things that you would do in those days. So I got to know him very well. He was always around and, like Charlie, a man with a lot of wisdom. He would always give you good advice and whether you took it or not was your business.

"I was around the Knock-na-Moe set-up for a couple of years. Then I had a disagreement with Charlie and went my own way. The hotel ran for a few years after that and Peter managed it, so it was not until some time in the early 90s that Peter came into my life again. Charlie had another business and Peter would have helped him out with that. It got to the stage where things started to get busier for me and I needed a driver. Peter was there, working with Charlie. We got talking and he said he would be interested, so I offered him the job.

"Ali was very friendly with Loretta, who works with Daniel O'Donnell," says Dominic. "We were playing at the Galtymore in London. She came along with Loretta. I remember her being introduced and I found that she was a teacher of home economics, which obviously includes all the seamstressing and sewing and that type of thing. I may have needed something done, like a pair of trousers taken up or whatever, and she offered to do it. She then started coming along to the shows and, lo and behold, before we knew it she was helping out. It's something now that's been going on for the last eight to ten years, and she does a fantastic job."

Of the selfless hours Ali spends driving herself all over the country, picking up the band's dirty washing and keeping them looking like stars, despite still holding down her teaching job, Dominic admits, "It's difficult to believe. Unfortunately, it's not a full time job. She has a job so, financially, she does well enough, and this doesn't cost her anything. She's looked after on the road. All her bills are paid and that kind of thing. But to have her on full time really wouldn't pay. But she knows that and we all respect her for it."

Dominic's second Eamon Campbell-produced album, *Evergreen,* followed closely the pattern of *Love Without End*, with the singer again backed by a lush curtain of swirling strings.

"We were trying to find a niche for Dominic in the market," says Campbell, "So you couldn't get too far away from the formula because the first album did quite well for him.

"But he sang that *Evergreen* brilliantly. I remember I was amazed at him singing that. There's some high notes at the end of that! And even *Release Me*. The key change. He just hit that - *Bang*! First time. Lots of other singers would have been struggling."

Amid the ballads, *Evergreen* also found Dominic tackling a couple of catchy, up tempo, 60s-style songs, *A Picture Of You* and *Hello Marylou*.

Mention of the latter brings a chuckle from Campbell. "I was actually singing the low bass line on that! Somewhere down in my boots!"

Musically, *Evergreen* may not have found Dominic breaking any ground that he hadn't covered on *Love Without End*. But, with gorgeously presented and warmly delivered songs like *The Only Couple On The Floor* and *Make The World Go Away*, it confirmed him as a hugely talented vocalist who deserved much wider recognition than he was getting from even the greatly expanded audience he was playing to at the time.

That such superlative albums as *Love Without End* and *Evergreen* didn't make Dominic's reputation overnight was simply due to the problem that has dogged him throughout his career and which has reduced the cultural impact of even Ritz's biggest seller, Daniel O'Donnell. The mainstream media in the UK, which makes instant household names out of so many minor pop stars and second rate TV personalities, steadfastly refuses to give house room to anyone connected to what it perceives as the unfashionable musical genres of country and easy listening.

While the American country stars of the 70s and 80s were allowed occasional UK chart hits in their time, even the superstars of Nashville couldn't get UK airplay and media coverage in the 90s unless, as in the case of Shania Twain, LeAnn Rimes and The Mavericks, they eradicated every trace of country from their sound. O'Donnell broke into the charts not because of any media support but simply because, through endless touring, he eventually built up a large enough fan base to buy his singles in sufficient quantities to chart.

What chance was there for a boy from Omagh who had yet to build up such a following?

Without mass market exposure to announce and celebrate his artistic achievements as they happened, Dominic had to take his music direct to his audience, spreading the word from venue to venue and building his reputation by word of mouth -and that takes time.

"The funny thing about *Evergreen*," reflects Dominic, "is that it was one of the first albums where I recognised that people were listening to my product. But it was only two years later, when we were down the road recording other albums, that it meant anything to our audience, because they never had the chance to listen to the words of the songs and, in particular, the ones they didn't know."

If they were released as new albums today, *Love Without End* and *Evergreen* would likely be hailed as Dominic's finest work and sell far more than they did. But, as Dominic points out: "At that time, we were probably ahead of our time in that our size of audience was not yet there."

That Dominic deserved a much higher profile in the world of entertainment was proven when he starred in and hosted *Sounds At The Sands*, a first- class series of music programmes made by Border Television.

"Border Television had shown an interest in doing a series of entertainment shows. Ritz were approached about it and I think they probably wanted Daniel to present the show, but he wasn't up for it. I don't know the politics of it, but it was then suggested to me that I present it, which was a great honour for me to do.

"When the eventual video and album came out, it was *Daniel & Friends,*" Dominic continues, "And, quite honestly, I understand why. Obviously it was to do with his popularity and his sales and stuff like that, so I didn't have a problem with that. I suppose they took a little bit of the limelight away from me, but it was no big deal."

But that was all later. The series that went to air was so good that it poses the question of why such a show doesn't exist on TV today. Recorded in a plush-looking concert situation at the Sands Centre in Carlisle, the format of the half hour programmes was astoundingly simple. Dominic would come on, sing a song or two, introduce his first guest, sing another song or two and then introduce a second guest, with everybody getting the chance to perform more than the one song that they would be allowed to present on any other show.

Naturally, Daniel O'Donnell closed the first programme with fellow Ritz artist Mary Duff appearing in a striking white lace mini-skirt earlier in the show.

"He hasn't done bad for a beginner. . ." quipped Dominic, introducing Daniel, who promptly replied, "It's good of Dominic to give us older singers a chance!"

The other guests brought a variety of musical styles to the series from 70s rocker Suzi Quatro and cockney pop stars Chas & Dave to Ritz artists like Tracy Elsdon and Sean O'Farrell, and

American soul legends The Drifters, with whom Dominic got to duet on *I'll Be There*.

The one black spot on the guest list was Elkie Brooks, who looked like Cruella de Ville during a gloomy jazz set on screen, and acted like it off stage -refusing even to shake Dominic's hand.

"I didn't have a great time with her," he admits, but, to his credit, refuses to enter into a slanging match.

"I ain't going down that road," the singer says gruffly. "I don't need to."

Dominic's own performances during the series displayed his versatility to great effect. Wearing a variety of colourful outfits, he switched effortlessly from the big ballad approach of *Noreen Bawn* to the rock'n'roll of *She's A Heartache*.

At one point, he burst onto the stage for a high-energy Irish medleyaccompanied by a wildly energetic display of Irish dancing. Tongue firmly in cheek, he even hung a medallion around his neck for a creditable version of Tom Jones' signature song, *It's Not Unusual*.

Although it was broadcast over a period of weeks, the entire series of *Sounds At The Sands* was made in two hectic days.

"They were done basically in concert format," says Dominic, "then I had to do links at certain times in front of the cameras. The big memories for me are of learning the scripts, the running back and forward, the changing of the outfits and the time between sets. It was a fun time and it was over too soon."

Had it been broadcast nationally in a prime slot, even on one of the secondary stations like BBC2 or Channel 4, it's easy to believe that the entertaining mix of music would have made *Sounds At The Sands* a hit with viewers. Unfortunately, that wasn't the case.

"In the Border region it went out at a respectable time. But then any networks that bought it, such as Ulster and RTE, put it out at two or three in the morning, so it didn't give the show much chance. People would come up and say, 'I saw you on TV last night,' so it was good to know people were up and about at that time, but it didn't get a lot of mainstream times.

"Looking back on the show I believe I carried it off reasonably well. I'd love to have another go at it , because I'd be a bit more relaxed about it now.

"It's always been talked about that it would be great to do again, but there's never been anything solid. This is what I believe is wrong with television. I think all aspects of variety entertainment should be given an opportunity through the media. But TV companies will tell you it's too expensive. They don't get the returns out of it that they need." ■

CHAPTER SEVEN

Through the Eyes of an Irishman

P HILOMENA BEGLEY insists: "It's not all glamour on the road." As if to prove the point, Ireland's Queen of Country is in the middle of making dinner for her family at her farmhouse in County Tyrone. She's in a hurry, because she's got a gig to do later. "People look at you and think you're making a fortune, but often you're spending more than you're making."

Cut to a dreary Friday lunchtime in Essex. Dominic is staying at the exotic- sounding Miami Hotel beside a noisy roundabout in not-so-exotic Chelmsford. Up for about an hour, having been driven through the night from the previous venue, Dominic finds a table for us in the small, otherwise deserted dining room-cum-bar.

"Are you sure you only want coffee?" He peers intently at the plastic menu. After much deliberation he settles on a Thai chicken dish. When it comes it's far from large. But, apart from some fruit, it's all the singer will eat before his show some seven hours later.

As he chats between mouthfuls, a sudden burst of traffic

noise announces the opening of the glass door from the street. Three women in their thirties come in with a couple of very young children and some small items of shopping. They exchange smiles and waves and hellos with the singer as they cross the small space to the bar. They're fans. Teachers, Dominic explains, who spend their half term breaks following Dominic from show to show. They stay at the same hotels, but don't hassle him, so he doesn't mind.

As if to prove the point, the group occupy a table in the corner behind Dominic. There's no staring or gawping. They just get on with their own conversation. Later, when he's finished his meal, Dominic will stroll over and pass the time of day. The group glances up, solemnly, at the TV on the wall where the lunchtime news is reporting the release from custody of the youths who killed James Bulger. Dominic gives the slightest, sad shake of his head. There's no difference between star and fans. It's just a group of friends in a hotel bar passing comment on the news of the day.

Unlike some artists who crave solitude, Dominic likes people around him. While he's eating, Peter McGlone and Jim McVeigh walk in. Jim is casual in a check shirt. McGlone, as always, is wearing a jacket and tie. As Jim goes to the bar to order some tea, Dominic waves Peter over to his table, his conspiratorial air inviting the older man to lean close.

"Behind the bar," Dominic says softly, nodding his head and barely moving his lips. "Who does she remind you of?"

Still leaning forward, McGlone looks up. "Oh!"

"The spitting image isn't she?" says Dominic, as the two enjoy a private joke. Dominic invites McGlone to join him at his table, but the assistant has calls to make on his mobile and excuses himself.

Dominic returns to an earnest conversation about his career. His concert schedule is as busy as ever. His new album, *Stone In Love With You*, is selling well. But Dominic considers himself at a crossroads. He wants to move on. He wants to get to the next level, but how? One thing he wants to do is move away from the Irish Singer tag. It's a logical decision since, on the mainland, Irish accents hardly predominate among his followers. That's why, on his current tour, he has dropped his Irish dancing routine, popular as it's always been.

"I mean," he reasons, leaning forward over his empty plate, "Tom Jones is Welsh, but you don't hear him singing about Wales all the time."

Be that as it may, ask Dominic's fans to name their favourite albums and many will say his fourth Ritz release, *Irish Favourites.*

The recording found Dominic back at the Homestead Studios in Randelstown, but with Shaun Wallace in the role of engineer while John McHugh, then the accordion player in Dominic's band, took the producer's seat assisted by Johnny Scott.

"The Irish Favourites started off as just being a live in-the-studio album with the same arrangements as he had on stage," recalls Wallace."It was then developed a bit and I think it actually turned out to be his biggest selling album. It did better than any he had done at that point.

"John McHugh started off working on the album. Basically he hadn't had that much studio experience, so we just asked Johnny to do some arrangement work on it. I did some arrangements on backing vocals and stuff."

With Eamon Campbell unavailable as a producer, due to increased commitments to The Dubliners, how did the relatively inexperienced McHugh come to be producing Dominic?

"It was the jobs for the boys syndrome," Dominic says bluntly. "It was always going to be a budget album. It was never going to be a top-class production, over the top album. So the record company at the time looked at it, like, 'We'll put so much money out for this album and we'll use whatever you have around you.' At that time, it was John McHugh.

"He'd done a lot of smaller time stuff," Dominic continues. "I don't mean that as a putdown, because everybody's album is important. But it probably hadn't gone beyond that small Irish market, you know?"

Of McHugh's ability as a producer, Dominic says, "I wouldn't put him down as a genius. He's a great musician. He's a man who plays four or five instruments. But it's horses for courses, really. You can watch people perform on stage and they're brilliant. But they can't put that down on tape. The creativity is not there. That's all I would say about John.

"The album came out and it did well," says Dominic, "But then, it was always going to do well, because it was Irish. I'm never going to be liked for saying this, but I really don't care, because I think it should have been better."

Despite Dominic's reservations about the producer, it's easy to see why *Irish Favourites* was a hit with his audience. Because of their familiarity with the material, both Dominic and the musicians sparkled on ballads like *Irish Eyes,* nimble foot-tappers like *The Star Of The County Down* and Irish nostalgia such as *If We Only Had Old Ireland Over Here.*

Among the highlights was a lively medley of *Patsy Fagan, Golden Jubilee, Mersheen Durkin, Courtin' In The Kitchen* and *It's A Great Day For The Irish* that Dominic would link with his Irish dancing on stage, and *A Sprig Of Irish Heather* – a waltz which would assume its own importance in Kirwan folklore.

My Galway Queen, meanwhile, was a perfect example of the genre known as country'n'Irish, the American country arrangement with lashings of steel guitar providing a wholly appropriate backdrop to a lyric about an Irishman who emigrates to America in search of fame and fortune but finds himself dreaming of his love back home.

The most interesting song on the album, however, was the opening *Through The Eyes Of An Irishman,* a superb, if unashamedly sentimental, evocation of Dominic's homeland, which fitted the singer like a glove. Although a new song, the lyric had the instantly classic feel of an anthem that had been passed down through the generations. Perhaps most surprisingly, for such a quintessential Irish song, it was written by cockney Terry Bradford.

"I wrote it because I've had a lot of experience in the Irish market," says Terry Bradford, soon to become Dominic's producer. "I've worked with a huge amount of Irish singers, going right back to when I wrote a song for the Nolan Sisters in 1979 or something. I worked with Joe Dolan. I got to meet The Fureys, and I've done a lot of writing and production for all of them over the years. Consequently, even though I've got no Irish connections whatsoever, I've been steeped in Irish music all the way down the line."

"Terry was very much part of the recording of the Phil Coulter material, *The Sea Of Tranquility* and all that kind of stuff," says Dominic. "He knows Irish music and the general approach to it. He has a good understanding of the content of Irish music and what people would like to listen to and look out for. I just think it's a rag he's an Englishman."

Of the song's origins, Bradford says, "I wanted to write one that was gonna kick around for a while. I looked at all the best Irish songs and I thought, 'What are the ingredients that make great Irish songs?'

"Certain things like they're quite long!" The songwriter answers himself with a laugh. "So I thought, you can get away with writing a long song, so then you can tell a better story. I wanted a really huge chorus that was gonna hit people inside and I just came up with this line, *'Through the eyes of an Irishman.'* Dunno where it came from. You just sit down and start writing a song and there it goes. It took me a long time to work on it. I thought it's really got to be something that touches people at the right place at the right time."

Several artists have since covered *Through the Eyes Of An Irishman*, but none has bettered Dominic's impassioned reading which quickly became a show-stopping part of his concerts.

Although many peple think that the song was written for Dominic, Bradford admits it was originally penned for Barry Owen who recorded the number. It made little or no impact and Gerry Crowley at Ritz wanted it for Dominic.

"Gerry said, 'We're not interested in Barry,' – which was no problem, because the deal with Barry had already been struck-"But we are interested in Dominic recording the song.'

"Now, it was a funny scenario, because it was a new song. We knew it had a life because of the reaction we'd had to it. I spoke to Barry and obviously, Barry was concerned that I was going to just say, 'Go ahead and do it.' All I said to Barry was, 'Once the record's out, there's very little that any of us can do about it.' Because once a song has been recorded it becomes available for other people to record, but before it's been recorded you need the publisher's consent – which was us. I was sort of put in a Catch 22 situation where I would have no say over it anyway, once it had gone out.

"Anyway, they said, 'Would you like to meet Dominic, blah, blah, blah. . .' And he made a very nice version of it. Now, Barry's record would have escaped, if that makes sense, from a label over in Ireland. Nothing was really done with it. But people took up on it with Dominic straight away. This happens sometimes with songs. As a result, people have always thought it was written for Dominic."

Looking back on *Irish Favourites*, Dominic says, "I suppose for what it was at the time, it was OK. It's one of those albums that will always be there and will always sell. It's very popular. I don't know what we sold on it, but it sold a lot.

"But it's not the type of Irish album I would do today. I would love to do another Irish album. It's something I want to do again. But I would have a completely different approach. I
Cont...d on page 135 ☞

Dominic in pensive mood.

Dominic on stage and in style.

On the road in Sydney, Australia with the crew and with musicians in Nashville, USA.

With Charlie Landsborough, another Ritz artist.

Producer Ronny Light at work with Dominic in the USA and in New Zealand with road manager Wally Bishop.

In Melbourne with radio presenter Keith McGowan and in Sydney Harbour with the famous Opera House in the background

With super stars Kenny Rogers and Suzy Quatro.

Friend and early manager Charlie McBrien. Below with Ricky Van Shelton.

126

The Kirwan family with Gloria Hunniford: Lee, Barry, Dominic, Jonathan, Louise and Colm. And below with Val Doonican.

Happy times with Vince Gill.

Snooker star John Virgo, Martine McCutcheon and Patrick Moore. And below with Sir Cliff Richard.

Tammy Wynette with Dominic.

Philomena Begley with Dominic.

John and Elizabeth Kirwan's wedding - August 4 1958.

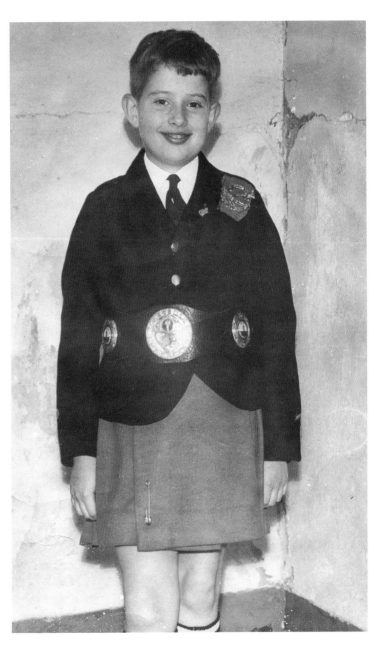

Dominic – a young star in the making.

Leaders of the Irish invasion Daniel O'Donnell and Dominic.

would make it more today's sound. The songs will always be there, and there's nothing wrong with them; I've grown up with those songs. But I'd look at my own arrangements. I can hear certain things in my head that would work better. I think there's so much more I could offer, and that's why I feel I could do a better one now."

Dominic's next album, *Today,* could not have been more different to *Irish Favourites* or, indeed, to his previous albums, being the first to link him with pop, rock and Latin sounds.

"We were trying to get to a different audience," says Mick Clerkin. "We appreciated the audience we had. But we were trying to broaden the audience; to do something more ambitious."

"I think they wanted to try something a bit more commercial, cross over-wise," says Shaun Wallace, who shared production duties on *Today* with Chris Harley. "It wasn't so country. We did it in quite a poppy way. That was probably because of what Chris and I had been doing just before the album. We were in a sort of pop mode, so we just kept going.

"It was quite strange because the *Irish Favourites* album and the *Today* album were started at the same time. We were working concurrently for some of the tracks on those."

Wallace says, "I think Dominic wanted to branch out and do more commercial stuff. But he knows where his success lies, so he's quite into the Irish stuff as well. He was probably hoping that he would broaden his horizons with the more pop stuff."

Dominic enjoyed recording the *Today* album using different ideas. "But it was probably slightly ahead of its time in what I really needed to be doing, because I was still being sold in a very easy-listening market. I think it took a while for *Today* to be accepted by the audience, although it has sold very well since. People have got used to the type of artist I am and they know that I can do this material."

Although Dominic enjoyed the musical diversity of the

sessions, the recording of *Today* did not run entirely smoothly. In his sleeve notes, Dominic writes, "A special word of thanks to my M.D. John McHugh for his help on the earlier part of the album," and, although he is not credited as a producer, *Today* was initially intended to be another McHugh production with Wallace in the engineer's seat.

In the event, Wallace was brought forward into the producer's role to take over what McHugh had begun. Then a third producer, Chris Harley, had to be recruited to complete the project.

"*Today*, if I remember correctly, was probably the most expensive album I ever recorded," says Dominic. "We hit hard times in the middle of it and there were conflicting attitudes between the personnel involved. It fell down in the middle and another producer had to be pulled in."

"They had a deadline," says Mudd. "I think it was three weeks to finish it, or something. I don't think I could have handled it myself that quickly, so I asked Chris to do it with me. We just got stuck in and worked around the clock for three weeks and got it done."

Filling in the background, Wallace explains: "Chris Harley is a producer from Scotland. I had been working with Chris on a band called The River Detectives from Glasgow. He was over here. He'd been doing a project, and the Dominic offer came up. I'd been working with Chris and I thought we could work well together on it. So I asked him to come in with me. Just, basically, because between the two of us we could play enough instruments and do enough backing vocals and stuff to finish the album."

The result of so many cooks in the kitchen was an album that was, stylistically all over the map, from the traditional country shuffle of *Someone Had To Teach You*, which had been a 1990 hit for George Strait, to the smouldering, Elvis-styled ballad *Little Things,* the frantic, horn-drenched rock'n'roll of *She's A*

Heartache and the contemporary styled pop-rock of *Another Saturday Night*.

On what could be viewed as either a commendable diversity or a woeful lack of direction on *Today* in particular and, to a lesser extent, Dominic's album career generally, the singer confides, "I don't think the record company ever got to know Dominic Kirwan. It's always been, 'Let's try this, let's try that, let's try the other. And I've been piggy in the middle.

"I'm probably as much to blame here. It stems really from my teenage years when I was in a band and played everything. I'm one of those guys who if somebody said, 'Here's a Bryan Adams song,' and I listened to it and thought, 'Yeah, I like that. I could do that on stage.' then I'd do it. That doesn't give critics, and it doesn't give audiences, and it doesn't give record companies a clear idea of what you are really about."

In mitigation, Dominic offers, "All I've ever asked for is for it to be accepted that I'm capable of being an entertainer."

The inspired opening cover of Sandie Shaw's 1965 chart topper *Long, Long Live Love* was unlike anything Dominic had ever recorded and was notable for introducing Dominic to a sunny, brassy, Latin sound that would prove popular with his fans throughout the coming years.

"There were a couple of Latin things," says Wallace, fondly. "I thought Dominic would be quite good at the type of thing that Ricky Martin does now. I thought that would be a good way for him to go. So we tried a lot of percussion. Almost like a Julio Iglesias up-tempo type thing. I think it suits him quite well. I think he could go more in that direction. Especially now, because it's quite popular in the mainstream.

"Dominic liked it, because it was different. He liked the idea of trying something new. He was into all that stuff," says Wallace.

Agreeing that he enjoyed the Latin direction of *Long, Long*

Live Love, Dominic turns to another song with a light, relaxing, tropical feel, *I'm Gonna Miss You Girl*.

"I love that track. I think that if I did that in the show today it would work. Because of that Latiny approach to some of the songs I do today, it's a today song. In fact, I've probably just jogged my memory and I'll play with that song in the next season.

"I've noticed, that when I bring back a song like *I'm Gonna Miss You Girl*, people go, 'Wow, what album was that on?' And my old albums start selling again. The back catalogue suddenly takes off. We've obviously recorded many, many good songs over the years and it's hard to get so many into the shows. So that's what I try to do."

Without a doubt, the finest of the country songs was the touching, story- telling ballad *Love Me*, which had been a recent American hit for Colin Raye. Significantly, it was the first time Dominic had cut a song by Skip Ewing, a Nashville songwriter to whom he would return time and again.

"I'm the sort who will cry at the drop of a hat," says Dominic, and the emotional singer dug deep into the touching lyric of love, old age and death, sounding at times close to tears as he sang, and doubtless salting the eyes of many who heard the album at home.

"Dominic can cry at the least little thing," confirms his friend and sponsor Kath McLarnon. "Just seeing a handicapped child, he'll fill up. Or even if he's watching the news and sees a child abused, you'll see tears in his eyes. He's very gentle like that. He's very soft like that. He's got a heart of gold."

Moving in yet another direction was the big and swinging *Your Such A Good Looking Woman*. With its funky percussion, profusion of horns and strings, and Trionagh Moore repeatedly singing the single line, 'Good looking woman,' the track was firmly after the style of Tom Jones.

"Very much," agrees Wallace. "Well, Dominic's show's like

that. So that was probably relating to his live show quite well. That was a huge arrangement. It had quite a lot of big strings. It was quite Latin I suppose. I think it was a bit more modern than the Joe Dolan version, which was quite Sixties and dated. I think we brought it up to date."

"That came from my earliest background," Dominic says. "Joe Dolan, an Irish act, had a real big hit with that. We changed the arrangement to make it more in the style of the time. It's not the same version that Joe did although his was probably more successful than mine. It was me putting a stamp on it my way."

Dominic also tackled the Garth Brooks hit *If Tomorrow Never Comes,* a powerful, romantic ballad in which the protagonist wonders if, in the event of being suddenly separated from his wife by tragedy, he would have done enough to let her know how much he loves her.

According to Wallace it was a "bit of a Chris Harley special. He did lots of backing vocals on that one, if I remember. At that stage I wasn't much into Garth Brooks. I hadn't listened to him that much, so I wasn't influenced by the original version. I remember thinking more along the lines of lots of strings and lots of backing vocals. We went more for a Beach Boys backing vocal sound."

Dominic was not impressed by the way the song was embellished.

"I think we should have stayed close to the original. What I try to do on stage is re-create what we do in the studios, and that's one track that I never even listened to. If I do *If Tomorrow Never Comes* on stage, it's closer to the Brooks version than my version. But we were trying for that little bit of crossover, you know? That was what we were looking for."

Returning to Wallace's production, generally, Dominic pauses before saying, "Mudd is a great guy and I've always enjoyed working in his studio. I think it's a great studio. But there's a little bit of self-indulgence that comes through. And a bit of not being capable of listening to other people. Because you can do something doesn't mean you have to do it. And I find that attitude has run through some of the albums from that particular studio. If they had stayed with the rawness and the pureness of what the original song was about then maybe the albums would have been more acceptable. There was a lot of, 'This is how I hear it, this is what you need to be doing today.' And in some cases that was wrong.

"I'm not afraid to say that today, but I was probably afraid to say it years ago. I didn't really know where I stood in the whole thing. I think if I had been a little more upstanding in what my thoughts were, we could have done better albums.

"I love the guy himself,. I think he's a very astute, intelligent guy who understands the whole industry. But I would say that listening to other people would be something that should be worked at."

As a teenager, Dominic was never much of a concert goer. "I think one of the first concerts I ever went to was when Simon & Garfunkle did their world arena tour. I was early married at the time and I remember going to see them in Dublin."

As his own career got underway, however, Dominic took the opportunity to see some of his fellow performers in action on his rare evenings off. Among them were Garth Brooks, Cliff Richard and, one of Dominic's personal heroes, Ricky Van Shelton. A meeting with the latter, he explains, gave him an understanding of how tongue-tied his own fans sometimes get when they meet him after a show.

"I've always been a big fan of Ricky . I just loved his voice. I liked that type of country singer. I couldn't see him in Ireland, when he came over to tour. The only place I could see him was in Glasgow, in the Pavillion Theatre where I have worked in myself. So, my wife and I took a weekend off, jumped on a flight, headed over and saw the show.

"I've never been that kind of guy who goes looking to speak

to the artist," Dominic adds, "I was more than grateful to see the man in action. I loved the show. But, on the way out, someone in the audience mentioned to the entourage that was with Ricky that I would like to meet him.

"When I met him I was in complete awe. I didn't know what to saw to this man! I was brought into the dressing room -one that I'd used myself- and it was a very strange feeling. . .

"In the previous year, I had seen Garth Brooks, Vince Gill. . . and Ricky. I loved all three shows. I liked everything about all of them, but each show was obviously very different.

"I'd been lucky enough to see Vince the previous year when he'd done a preview spot at the Jazz Cafe in London, and I loved every aspect of that. So, when Vince came on tour with his band, because I'm a vocalist, it was his voice I wanted to hear. It was the songs I wanted to hear. I can respect the instrumental parts of a show, of course I can. Unfortunately for me, when Vince came, there was too much guitar, so he sort of let me down a bit. Then, Garth Brooks: One hell of a show. I saw him at The Point in Dublin. But, to me, it was just Hollywood on wings. If you had taken away all the trappings and the trimmings, then I would have liked the show.

"But when I saw Ricky it was pure rawness, and because it was raw, I thought it was the best show of the lot. So, when I met him, I came out with some sort of statement like: 'I'm pleased to meet you. God, I've seen three shows this year and you've been the best of them all!'

"I realised that was a stupid statement," Dominic laughs, "but I was just in awe of the man."

Despite that statement, Dominic admits he has never exhibited the kind of obsession with a performer that many of his fans have for him.

"I might want to see an act or a show and I go along and maybe I might think about going back to see it again at a later date. But I don't go back the next 20 nights."

As for not attending many concerts in his youth, Dominic says, "I don't regret it. And yet I think it's a good thing for a singer to do. I think you should watch other people. You should watch stage settings, lighting. The little bits of magic they create. After that, I think you should put it all in the back of your head and then be yourself. It's all about being an individual."

Turning to the artists he has worked with as a support act, Dominic says, "The one I got to know the closest, as in being able to talk to him and relate to him, was Charley Pride. Ever since that year, we've always had a Christmas card from him. I've met him twice since then, once in Nashville, and when you walk into the room he just knows you immediately. I think that speaks volumes.

"The biggest lesson I learned from Charley was no matter who you are and how big an act you are, it's a very simple thing to go along to the support act and say, 'Hello and welcome to the show,' and hopefully treat them as you'd like people to be treating you. Charley Pride was like that. He taught me that.

"We talked a little about his early days, that voice on the radio without a face, but the way things changed for him over the years when people eventually knew he was a black country singer. But he's not bitter about it. If anything, he gets a laugh out of it. He's a very funny man. He enjoys a laugh. I found him a very good man. A very good person."

Tammy Wynette, by contrast, was more remote.

"We never really got to know Tammy. We met her, we had photographs taken, but we never got to spend much time with her, which was unfortunate. She wasn't well. But the little brief time that we met her, I found her pleasant . We were with her at the time she was recording with KLF. She was on the charts. She was on *Top Of The Pops*. There was definitely a lot more media attention.

"The Kenny Rogers tour was only for six shows, but it was a

real experience to meet him and to watch him on stage. Had it lasted for more than six shows we probably would have had some time together. But the time we were there, we were well looked after. Everybody respected each other.

"I think what came through most on all these tours, was that once the Americans felt that these guys are serious about what we do, we got respect. I think over the years, with a lot of these people, promoters put on opening acts that didn't care. They didn't try to do anything. Whereas we were wanting to get out there, we were wanting to do it professionally, we were wanting to do our sound checks, we were wanting to do right for the show. I think that was recognised at a very early stage and, once it was, everyone was relaxed and got on."

As Dominic's popularity grew, he became the headliner used by Ritz to launch the careers of other acts, such as Sarah Jory and Tracy Elsdon.

The final song on *Today* was a duet with Elsdon on *I'll Walk Beside You*. Unlike the rest of the tracks on the album, the song was produced by its writer, Terry Bradford, and sign-posted the beginning of a new era in Dominic's recording career. ■

CHAPTER EIGHT

On the Way to a Dream

"WE WERE working to a plan to make Dominic a national star," says Bradford. It was a plan that might have worked had everybody pulled in the same direction.

As one of the chief architects behind Dominic's bid for stardom, Bradford took over the producer's seat for Dominic's sixth album, *On The Way To A Dream*. It was a position Bradford had wanted to occupy since Dominic recorded Bradford's song *Through The Eyes Of An Irishman* on *Irish Favourites*. At the time, Bradford had travelled to Scotland at the invitation of Ritz A&R man Gerry Crowley to see Dominic in concert.

"When I first saw Dominic it was obvious to me that he had something special," says Terry in an East London accent uncompromised by years of exile in Birmingham where his studio, The Famous Music Company, is based. "I've been in the business for many, many years, and you get to sniff when somebody has really got it."

Bradford defines the star quality that he saw in Dominic. "He didn't have to try very hard. Some people try desperately on stage to be liked. Some people do everything they can to be noticed. Dominic didn't have to do either. He's a very likeable character. He's got a charismatic quality. People are drawn to him.

"One of his great attributes is that people like him. In this game there are a lot of people who have unfortunate manners and people just don't like 'em. But Dominic's the opposite. He's a very likeable man.

"I was with Susie, my other half. We both looked at each other and said, 'This bloke should be doing something serious.' And I said to Gerry, 'I would very much like to get involved with him musically.' Rather than just write a song, I wanted to produce him."

At the time, Bradford was producing his first album for Ritz with Tracy Elsdon. As Tracy was opening Dominic's shows at the time, it was an entirely logical move to invite Dominic to duet with Tracy on Bradford's composition *I'll Walk Beside You*. Artistically, the recording was a complete success and, as well as appearing on Tracy's debut album, which became the first Ritz album to be playlisted on Radio 2, the track was used to close Dominic's album, *Today*, where it proved to be one of the most pleasing numbers.

When it came to choosing the producer for Dominic's next album, Bradford was the obvious choice. He recalls the brief he was given when Ritz gave him the job.

"Mick Clerkin and Gerry Crowley came to the studio and said, 'We want to do an album like Michael Bolton. We want to turn Dominic into a sort of rougher edged thing.'"

"I'm not a big Michael Bolton fan," says Dominic, interviewed separately. "I mean, I know what he does. I have listened to him and I know what they meant. But I'm still not in that major vocal range."

Bradford felt the same way.

"I'd listened to all Dominic's albums by then and got to know him quite well. So I said to them, 'You're not running before you can walk are you? I know we've got to make it perhaps a little bit more contemporary to get the radios interested,' Because radio and TV want something contemporary. 'But is it not a little too fast? Maybe it could be halfway house?' Anyway, after a lot of talking they agreed that maybe they were trying to be a little bit ambitious by going the whole hog. So we settled on a halfway slot.

"We ended up with an album that was just down the middle and the reaction from the radios was probably the strongest that Dominic's ever had."

From the word go, it was intended that *On The Way To A Dream* would comprise mainly new material.

"I had recorded five albums at that time," Dominic recalls. "I think the record company were looking for something that would give me a bit more direction in what I was doing as an artist, and also to stretch out further to a wider audience. It probably didn't set the world on fire, but it did make people sit up and look at me as an artist."

Bradford believes that at that time Dominic was happy to go anywhere that could lead to some sort of success.

"I'm not saying he didn't have any input, because with all the songs we'd say, 'Have a listen to these, do you like these?' Myself, Gerry Crowley and Mick Clerkin, mainly, and Dominic, had the say on what the final songs would be. Dominic had to like the songs. He had to enjoy the songs. And he picked a lot of the songs anyway."

Bradford ended up writing six of the selections, including four co-written with his partner Susie Arvesen. Some of them were specifically written with Dominic in mind. The title track, *On The Way To A Dream*, however, was written for song and dance man Gary Wilmot.

"I did an album with Gary and I wasn't completely pleased," reflects Bradford. "I felt I could have done a better job. I think I could have done more with him. Gary's album came and went. Nothing happened with it at all. So I was sitting on what I thought were one or two very strong songs. Another one on there which we did with Dominic was *I Won't Forget You*.

They're quite hard songs to sing, and Dominic did a great job on both of them.

"The record company decided they'd use *On The Way To A Dream* as the title track and it was a good title for Dominic as he was starting a new career in a sense. He was coming into this new, more success-oriented direction."

One of the songs specifically written with Dominic in mind was the opening track, *Where Does Love Go When It Dies*. It was a soulful, power ballad, intro'd with a modern sounding sax and distinguished by stirring melodic surges and contrasting, compelling, breath-catching pauses. Dominic delivered a scorching performance.

"That was a song that I picked." says Dominic, firmly, "It's a very powerful song. If you gave some of Bradford's songs to some of the more mainstream pop artists, with the media attention that they'd get, I'd say there would be a few songs on that album that would have been hits.

"Here I was, an unknown Irish artist – well, not completely unknown, but unknown to the greater media – and it was probably more of an uphill battle to get the breaks and opportunities and have major success. But I believe there are some really good songs in there capable of being big successes for the right people."

Of the few covers on the album, Dominic as always had an eye on the current American country charts. In this instance he picked Hal Ketchum's catchy, mid-tempo hit *Tonight We Might Just Fall In Love Again*, commenting, "Terry's changed it slightly in the arrangement. But it's a good song and it works great in a live show."

There were also a couple of songs from Skip Ewing, who was fast becoming Dominic's favourite Nashville writer. *Our Love* was a likeable, bouncy, foot-tapper which Bradford removed somewhat from its obvious country origins and moved closer to the pop sound of the rest of the album with the addition of a buzzy electric guitar and organ style keyboards. *Someone In Your Eyes* was a slow, soulful ballad that followed closely the pattern established by the album's opener, *Where Does Love Go When It Dies*.

Again, Dominic turned in an excellent performance, his voice taking on a darker, heavier, raspier hue than on previous albums. Michael Bolton he might not have been, but he had certainly distanced himself from the lilting country'n'Irish sound of most of his fellow Ritz artists. And, of course, he commanded a frenzied loyalty in his fans that Bolton would have swapped his long curly hair for.

The most enduring song from the album in terms of Dominic's concert career was *The Answer To Everything*. On stage the song has become an audience participation favourite with Dominic's fans delighting in repeatedly shouting 'Yes!' to Dominic's 'Do you love me?'

"People were just going to jump on certain words of it," smiles the singer. "I suppose it gave us a good buzz and a good feeling. The fans liked the words and they wanted the opportunity to participate, and here was a song they could participate in."

Listened to on disc, however, without an audience response, it becomes apparent that Burt Bacharach and Hal David's lyric is a far stronger piece of material than the throwaway novelty it might appear in a live concert. It is a beautifully written ballad that Dominic delivers with passion. Although he clearly enjoys the ritual that *The Answer To Everything* has become, does he feel that the treatment has actually taken something from the song?

"It's a very good song. It has the standing of being a good single. So, yes, there is a part that is taken away, particularly for people who want to go and watch a show and listen to words. But it's become part of it now and I suppose people recognise that."

Perhaps the most unusual cover Dominic has ever recorded

was the Robbie Burns poem *My Love Is Like A Red, Red Rose*, which Bradford set to music.

"One of the main reasons it was recorded was we were doing a lot of work in Scotland and we thought we should do a Scottish song," says Dominic.

Bradford enjoys working with Dominic. "Dominic has always been very easy. He took direction. He was quite happy to be produced. When you're producing an album the worst thing in the world is when you're fighting people all the time. But Dominic was really, really buzzing. He liked the way the tracks were coming together. He liked the way the sound was developing. He was happy on all sides. Well, that's what he let me believe, anyway! He's certainly not a prima donna, so that was the nicest part. He's a hard worker."

"Terry is a slow worker," says Dominic. "I don't mean that in any uncomplimentary way. He'll tell you that himself."

"I'm probably the world's slowest producer in album terms," chuckles Bradford.

"So it was a few months from start to finish," says Dominic. "It was generally only a song a day that Terry would work with. Rarely did you ever get two songs done in a day. So we'd maybe do two or three songs in a week and then go back a fortnight later."

"It was very enjoyable," says Bradford.

The most important part of the production process for Bradford was getting the best out of Dominic's voice.

"I suppose I'm dictatorial. I know what I want to hear from a singer and I work extremely hard to get that. I don't care if it takes one time through or if it takes analysing every word. The be all and end all for me is that when a singer sings a vocal it's got to be that they walk out of the studio thinking 'I could not do any better than that.'

"One of the first things I said to Dominic was, 'You've got to think about the words that you're singing.' If there was anything I felt with Dominic it was that he had this soaring voice and it was all natural, God-given charisma, and yet it wasn't wrapped up very well. Sometimes people have it and they don't realise what they've got. Dominic was lucky enough to have all these things and, as I say, he didn't have to try very hard for this charismatic thing to come across.

"So all I kept on saying to him was, 'Sometimes people like to see people giving it a little bit more. Thinking about the lyrics. Making the lyrics work.' Tunes are tunes and obviously if you get a good melody people are going to like it, but the right performance on the right word can make the difference between the hairs standing up on the back of people's necks, or just being lost.

"The only thing I was ever saying to Dominic was, 'Think about the lyrics. Think, think, think. And form the lyrics at all times.' Because you've only got one chance. The record's on and then it's gone. That goes for audiences and it goes for the radio stations."

It was a lesson well learned by the singer.

"Terry Bradford was a turning point in my life,. He worked very, very hard with me on the voice on the performance. Hence now when I go into studios I am a lot more exact. When I hear recordings by other acts and I know they haven't done their homework on their vocal, I sometimes cringe. That's only because people like Terry have made me more aware of it."

The reaction to *On The Way To A Dream* was as good as anyone could have wished for. In fact, it was overwhelming.

"The album was play-listed on Radio 2," recalls Bradford. "I remember Mick Clerkin coming over to me while we were in Ireland. He came beaming up to me: 'We've just had it play-listed on Radio 2. First time ever!' Ironically, the first time anything on Ritz had been play-listed was the album I did on Tracy Elsdon. They play-listed a track called *Half The Moon* and it was played for 11 weeks. That had never been heard of for

Ritz. Not Daniel. None of them had ever had play-listing. But Dominic's album, as an album, was the first album that had ever been play-listed. Clerkin was absolutely jumping. We all were. 'Course we all were. It was fantastic."

As well as playing the music, radio stations were quick to interview the singer. Television exposure also followed.

Three of the songs from *On The Way To A Dream* were showcased on Grampian TV's *Scotch & Irish* programme, which devoted a full thirty-minute show to Dominic and Tracy Elsdon. Opening with the bouncy *Tonight We Might Just Fall In Love Again*, Dominic introduced the show before going into a striking reading of *Where Does Love Go When It Dies*. Sharply dressed in a dark blue suit and checkerboard shirt, Dominic also sang a moving *Hands Across The Ocean*.

The climax of the show, in every sense, however, was the closing duet with Tracy Elsdon from their earlier recording, *I'll Walk Beside You*. Elsdon was one of those rare singers who was also a consummate actress. In addition to a haunting, enigmatic voice, she was blessed with a pair of huge, captivating eyes and the ability to make every word she sang completely believable with the smallest glance, smile or tilt of her attractive head.

Slender and ravishing in a long, tight black dress, with those enormous eyes never leaving her duet partner, she looked every inch the adoring lover that she was playing in the song. When she and Dominic clasped hands for the line, "Take my hand... I'll satisfy you," it was a wonder the sexual frisson she generated didn't short circuit the TV cameras. Even Dominic, renowned as he was for flirting with his audience, didn't seem quite sure where to look, and adopted a goofy smile for a more light-hearted reading of his half of the song. But when he put his arm around Elsdon for a final, friendly squeeze as the final notes died away and the applause broke out, they made an enchanting couple.

Watching what may have been Elsdon's final television

performance, seeing how the camera loved her and how she made herself and the song as one, it is easy to believe that she could have become the biggest star Ritz ever recorded. The slightly remote, haunted air that gave the singer her allure, however, was no mere stage affection. Tracy wasn't happy and withdrew from the music business soon after. Reputedly unable to cope with the pressure as fame beckoned, her huge potential was never realised.

Far keener to embrace adulation, Dominic returned to *Scotch & Irish* within a couple of weeks. Wearing a red suit he might have borrowed from either Tom Jones or a Harlem crack dealer, he sang the rousing Terry Bradford song *We'll Be Together From Now On* from *On The Way To A Dream* and, perhaps more in keeping with the original musical intentions of the show, the foot-tapping country'n'Irish song *Tipperary On My Mind* from *Irish Favourites*. Later in the programme he reaffirmed his commitment to his Scottish fans by changing into a kilt to sing a medley of *Donald Where's Your Troosers* and *My Bonnie Lies Over The Ocean*. The performance fitted no part of Bradford's plan to make Dominic a national star, but the singer was never one to limit his musical agenda.

A far more important television breakthrough for Dominic was the first of two appearances on the BBC's top-rated daytime show *Pebble Mill*. It was arranged by Mike Perry of MP Promotions, who had been brought into the Ritz team by Bradford to help promote Dominic on TV and radio

"I worked with Terry in the 70s, when he was in the group Coco in the Eurovision song contest," Perry remembers, "We lost touch a little bit. Then, I was doing some work with *Pebble Mill* and one of the girls was married to a backing singer. She happened to mention Terry Bradford and I said, 'Oh, I know Terry...' So I went to see Terry at his studio in Bromsgrove, talked about old times, and he said, 'Look, I'm doing this album with Dominic Kirwan. He's an artist I think you'd enjoy looking after and promoting.' I got Dominic some TV appearances on *Pebble Mill* and it started from there."

At the top of the programme, presenter Alan Tichmarsh promised, "We'll be hearing from new Irish sensation Dominic Kirwan," and the roar from the studio audience let it be known that the DK fan club were out in force.

"He's not *that* sensational," joked Tichmarsh, only to be forced by more hollers to concede, "All right, he is!"

When Dominic finally made his appearance to sing *Where Does Love Go When It Dies*, he looked undeniably and understandably nervous. But he controlled it well and put the song across with class.

"In fact we had to do it again, because Dominic made a little mistake," says Perry, "So we did the song twice -which the audience loved."

Terry Bradford, one of a quartet of backing singers, looked as though he was having the time of his life, visibly basking in the glow of a star on the ascent.

"We had massive shows at that time," says Bradford, "and it was the first time Dominic had been anywhere near that sort of exposure. He was brilliant. He handled himself extremely professionally. Everybody was buzzing. It was electric. It was a very, very interesting time."

In fact, so well received was Dominic's appearance on Pebble Mill that he was asked to return, this time for an in depth interview with Sarah Greene.

"It was about a ten minute piece, a very major piece," says Perry. "She was like, 'Oh, you're a really big star and you're doing all these tours and concerts.' He still feels it's one of the best interviews he ever did. It was a very good piece."

"That was the biggest national show I'd done. I felt very good. That was the time that the young band Take That were breaking up and there was an opportunity where we stepped in. I suppose I was very nervous about the whole thing. It has to be the most major show I did at the time, and to be able to sit down and be interviewed by somebody as popular and known throughout the nation as Sarah... I was nervous. But she was very relaxing. We seemed to hit it off. A lot of people have told me the interview was excellent.

"So, after that, I thought, 'OK, you've done this once. It shouldn't be any problem doing it again.' Unfortunately, we didn't get too many opportunities after that."

Dominic did, however, make an accomplished appearance on Grampian TV's Art Sutter Show. Dressed in tweed jacket and waistcoat, coupled with black trousers, he opened with the album track *Northern Lights Are Shining On Me*. From the illuminated plastic candles swaying in the studio audience it was clear that, once again, he had brought his fan club with him.

In the interview that followed, Sutter told the audience that Dominic's album, *On The Way To A Dream*, had hit number one on the country charts. The talk also turned to Dominic's background as an Irish dancer. "You could have been Michael Flatley in *Riverdance*," joked Sutter, adding, "You could have been *Dominic Kirwan* in *Riverdance!*"

Dominic briefly explained the difference between the basic traditional dancing he did and the more complex affair with which Flatley had made his name. Then, to the delight of the studio audience, he needed little bidding to strip off his jacket and give a brief but spirited demonstration of his nifty footwork.

To close the show, Dominic returned to sing *The Answer To Everything*. He couldn't resist a smile as he sang the line, "Do you love me?" Any shouts of "Yes!" from the studio audience never reached the viewers at home but the sharper eyed would have seen the word clearly mouthed by several present. They also would have seen the pitched excitement when, in a faithful recreation of his stage show, Dominic walked up the steps among the faithful and exchanged countless kisses for an armful of roses.

In every way it was a wonderful moment of television that deserved far wider exposure than its regional daytime slot.

Similarly, although it topped the British country charts, *On The Way To A Dream* deserved better than to fall just outside of the pop Top 75. That the album missed the 75 by just 30 copies seems a particularly cruel twist of fate.

"We were incredibly unlucky," says Bradford. "When you get in the 75, you're featured in *Music Week* and all the windows of Woolworths and all the rest of it. But, unfortunately, it was 30 copies outside. We were all hoping for Dominic's album to do something. Then we got a call to say Dominic's album was something like number 50 midweek."

"What goes through your mind," says Dominic, "is, 'good Lord, you're in the charts! The national charts!' You have to feel good about that."

"It was unbelievable news. We were so up," says Bradford.

"Obviously I was on tenterhooks about how it was going to end up at the end of the week," says Dominic.

But by the end of the week Bradford received a phone call to say it had fallen to 76.

The midweek chart positions, which are not released to the public and which are closely guarded within the music industry, are always different from the final published chart, partly because teenagers, who represent the largest part of the record buying market, traditionally make their purchases towards the end of the week on Friday and Saturday.

As a result, the records aimed at teenagers may sell relatively sluggishly at the beginning of the week and perform less well on the midweek chart than they do on the actual chart. The midweek chart does, however, give record companies an indication of which records are selling quickly and which they should put every promotional effort behind in a bid to secure a high chart placing. The charts, after all, don't merely monitor the success of a record, they also stimulate it. The higher a record climbs on the charts, the more attention and exposure it gets and the more it is likely to sell. The position in which a record first enters the chart is particularly crucial in determining which artists the radio stations deem popular enough for airplay.

Knowing they had a potential hit on their hands, could Ritz have done more in the limited time available to prevent *On The Way To A Dream* sliding from 50 to 76 between Thursday and Saturday?

Mike Perry explains, "Ritz didn't have what we call a strike force, which is like a team of guys going into all the chart shops, putting the single in and making sure they've got stock. They were more geared to album sales than the charts. So he didn't get the breakthrough. But I know in radio terms it was an album that was very well accepted. A lot of people think it's one of the best things Dominic ever did, radio-wise. A lot of radio stations played it. It gave us a bit of credibility and a bit of legs on that one."

Perhaps one reason Ritz didn't, or couldn't, do more for Dominic was that the company already had an unexpected hit on its hands in the form of Liverpool school teacher Charlie Landsborough who had captured the imagination of easy listening fans all over the UK and Ireland with his gentle, now classic, song about a blind boy who asks his father the heart wrenching titular question, *What Colour Is The Wind?*

Clerkin admitted: "We had one album with Charlie through my relationship with Tony Allan. Foster & Allen had left to go to Telstar. They used to take artists developed by people like us and advertise them on television. They don't do it anymore. I couldn't offer them the money that Telstar were offering. So we left it. I said, 'Fine guys. OK. I wish you the best of luck, and off you go.' We remained good friends. Still do.

"Tony was a good friend of Charlie's, because Charlie had written a couple of hits for them. He recorded an album with Charlie called *Songs Of The Heart*. Tony phoned me up and asked if I'd be interested in putting it out. So I said, 'Send it to me and I'll have a listen.' I thought it was quite pleasant and all, so we put that one out. Then, we were talking about another one and Charlie said to Tony, 'Why don't I go and talk to Mick direct? No disrespect, but what's the point in me going to you and you going to Mick?' So Charlie contacted me direct and I said, 'Sure, fine, I'll go with it.' That was the *What Colour Is The Wind* album. It was around for about three months and nothing much was happening. Then he got a couple of breaks on television here in Ireland. It was a case of being in the right place at the right time and the rest, as they say, is history. It just took off, big time."

"Out of the blue, Charlie's album went straight to Number One in Ireland." says Bradford. "It went crazy. He did a TV show over there and it just took off like a rocket. That was a shame for Dominic because suddenly the record company's attention was divided. You can't blame anyone for that, other than the fact that Charlie's album was happening in a big way. We were all jumping up and down. 'You've got to get behind it, you've got to get behind it,' and there's only so much, I suppose, that a record company can do at any given time."

Ironically, Charlie's album was also produced by the ubiquitous Terry Bradford. Although Landsborough had written one of the chart hits upon which Ritz was founded when Foster & Allen recorded his *I Will Love You All My Life,* which had since become an MOR standard, nobody expected the gifted but unassuming songwriter to become a successful artist. Least of all, Charlie.

"I don't think he had any more ideas that he'd be successful than fly in the air," smiles Bradford. "But the thing that amazed me was the first time he came in and opened his mouth. His voice...

"To be completely honest, the record company said to me, 'Go and make an album with Charlie. Don't worry about how it comes out.' Not in those words. But what they did say was, 'We're interested in his songs. We're obligated to make an album. We said we'd make it. So go and make it. Don't worry about it too much.'

"When I heard this voice coming out, I went straight back to the record company and said, 'Do you realise you've got this monster singer 'ere?' And, of course, when the album was made, they were all jumping up and down. It came out and it didn't do anything. Then he did this TV show in Ireland and became an overnight success. That album would have been a Top Ten album in the mainstream in England, but it was a mid-price album, so it was number six in the Mid Price Top Ten."

Although, as the producer, he was delighted at Landsborough's success, Bradford admits, "I felt really sorry for Dominic at that time. We'd been working so hard on his album. Suddenly Charlie came along and stole his thunder. The record company can really only go one route. They have to gravitate towards the success straight away. I'm not saying they didn't do anything for Dominic, because they did, but the timing could have been better.

"I was actually in Ireland with Charlie when we got the call to say *On The Way To A Dream* was 50 midweek. I thought everybody should have put everything behind it because not only would they have had Daniel successful, they had Charlie successful and they would have had a third artist. I felt really sorry for Dominic because he was behind Daniel at that point and suddenly he was shanghaied by Charlie Landsborough.

"The one upside was that *On The Way To A Dream* went to Number One on the British country charts. Then we did the video with him at the Rialto and I think that went to Number 17 on the video charts. There was a lot of hard work on all sides and I think it paid off."

Perry agrees that because of Landsborough and others

Dominic did not get the maximum support of Ritz at the time when he was closest to a national breakthrough.

"Charlie was very hot that first couple of years. So he did tend to take over a little bit. And obviously you've got Daniel who is always there doing well. He's the No. 1 act at Ritz, of course.

"I think the other thing Dominic suffered was that they signed Mark Roberts, who came second in Eurovision. Also, they signed Michael English, who was going to be the new Daniel O'Donnell. So there was an 18-month period when Dominic's career suffered. He didn't seem to get the backing or support that perhaps he should have. There wasn't the input in the creative side. I think he lacked a bit of direction, really."

Mick Clerkin, however, refutes the suggestion that Dominic suffered because of Landsborough's success.

"I wouldn't accept that. We have always looked at each and every artist as a priority. We try and avoid bringing out product at the same time, so we can pay attention to the one artist that we're dealing with at that particular time. They were different types of artist, anyway. Different audience, I thought.

"I would avoid having two artists that were similar. That's why I didn't think there was much similarity between Daniel and Dominic. Dominic was more aggressive. A Tony Christie, Tom Jones type of performer. Charlie was very laid back. He just sat there and played his guitar. He told his stories. He was a totally different kind of act in my estimation. So I don't really think there was any conflict there at all."

Ironically, Perry reports that "Mark Roberts did absolutely nothing. He's got no fan base. He just happened to come second in Eurovision and they signed him on the basis of that."

Teenage singer Michael English, meanwhile, found himself playing to tiny audiences on an interminable, hugely misjudged and over-ambitious debut UK theatre tour when he should have been building his fan base, as Dominic had years earlier, playing support to established acts.

"Michael English is not Daniel O'Donnell and I think it was wrong to market him that way," says Perry. "I think he's gonna do his own thing. He plays keyboards and he's more of a singer-songwriter. But, yes, Dominic did suffer during that period."

Despite seeing his record company's efforts directed to less worthy artists while his own opportunities seemed to be slipping by, Dominic expressed no resentment towards his fellow artists on the label.

"He likes them all," says Perry. "I think he knew some of the attention was going on Charlie, and obviously some of the money, but he's never cynical or bitter about it."

Asked about Landsborough's success, Dominic says, "Charlie, of course, was the support to me when he went to Number One in Ireland and, fair play to him, he stood by his commitment. He was supporting me at the Opera House in Belfast and another couple of shows locally and he'd just gone to Number One the week he did that. So I respect Charlie a lot."

As for his own thoughts on the chart performance of *On The Way To A Dream*, Dominic says, "Terry feels there wasn't enough general publicity done with the album at the time to get it that little bit further. I don't know. I'm not too deeply into all that. He feels it could have gone a bit further if it had been given more opportunity. But it was still a good feeling at the time to know that you had charted." ■

CHAPTER NINE

It's all in the Game

TWO YEARS passed between the release of *On The Way To A Dream* and Dominic's next Bradford-helmed release. In the sleeve notes to *The Music's Back*, the singer revealed that he'd had "some anxious moments" in the interim. Basically, Dominic's intensive, unrelenting schedule had finally caught up with him. His voice would take no more.

"One of the problems when you're on the road all the time is everything about the road is dreadful," sighs Bradford. "It's very hard to live a healthy lifestyle when you're travelling around in cars and vans and so on. You're stopping in garages and eating rubbish. And, of course, Dominic has a very active audience. A very vocal audience. So, consequently, he's doing a two-hour show and then he's standing afterwards talking to everybody for two hours.

"Now, we always told Dominic to be very careful, because the damage to voices is not done when you sing. If you sing correctly you should not damage your voice. But if you stand and talk for two or three hours afterwards then you'll do more damage in the first half hour of that than you will in three hours of singing."

Of the time Dominic devotes to his fans after every show,

promoter Stewart Laurie says, "Other artists like Mary Duff would spend a lot of time. Daniel would spend a lot of time. But none would spend the amount of time that Dominic does. There are times when I've seen him leave a hall at three o'clock in the morning.

"Joe Dolan could spend time and do it well, but do it quickly," Laurie continues. "But that came through experience. Joe Dolan's a man of 60. Dominic's his own worst enemy in the autograph queue because he has too much to say at times. He gets carried away with it and can't hold himself back. When he gets into the car at the end of the night he's on a high after speaking to these people."

"Basically he'd overdone it. It's as simple as that," says Bradford. "He'd worked morning, noon and night, dashing around doing this, that and the other. The body gets a little bit rundown. The first thing that happens is your throat dries up. If you have a row with someone, with most people their throat dries up and their voice changes slightly. Now, if you're performing four or five times a week and you've not got a very healthy lifestyle, you're at risk from everything that comes along."

It was Bradford who first noticed the problem.

"We came to the point where we had three or four aborted recording sessions. I've always been into voices. Susie is as well. So I told Dominic I could detect a little something in his voice and if he didn't look after it there would be a problem."

"I had been under a lot of pressure," says Dominic. "Work was getting greater. I was doing a lot of shows. I was feeling tired and stressed. I went to the studio and started to work on the album and Terry spotted the problem.

"Luckily, Terry had a contact in Birmingham called Paul Farrington who is a voice specialist."

"Paul Farrington is actually Susie's singing teacher and Paul, within an hour, had him down at the surgeon's with a camera down his throat." says Bradford.

"I went there at about 4 o'clock in the afternoon and he referred me to a surgeon in the Queen Elizabeth Hospital, Birmingham. He agreed to see me at about seven o'clock that evening. I had a private appointment."

"David Proops is one of the most eminent surgeons in the world." says Bradford. "He's worked with loads of actors and singers. He's very, very knowledgeable. A nice guy as well."

"He did the whole lot," says Dominic. "The camera down the throat and whatever. Luckily, they were able to tell me that I had no major damage to my vocal chords, but my muscles were showing a lot of stress. The immediate advice was just to sit back.and rest for ten days.

"David said, 'You don't have anything wrong, but you do have a very inflamed set of vocal chords which will only get better by rest.'" says Bradford. "He said Dominic needed ten days rest and over. And that's what happened."

"Of course it was worrying. But if anything I was relieved that it was all happening so fast," says Dominic. "I took a couple of weeks break. I rested my voice. Then I started working with Paul. He showed me some ways of voice exercising and basically looking after my voice. I've been doing that ever since and it definitely seems to have restored it."

Even given the rest and subsequent vocal training, it is impossible to miss the wear in the voice that Dominic displays on *The Music's Back*. Although Bradford attributes the vocal style in part to an attempt to "give him a slightly rougher, more contemporary sound," Dominic's voice sounds less flexible than it did on earlier recordings. He spends much of his time in a husky, throaty, lower register and although he still hits the high notes -particularly at the close of an impassioned *I Swear*-the strain is frequently painfully evident. Playing the album back to back with the beautiful, soaring and effortless sounds that Dominic displayed on his Eamon Campbell produced albums, *Love Without End* and *Evergreen*, the deterioration in the timbre of the Kirwan voice over such a short period is little short of shocking.

"But then he was gigging a tremendous amount and his voice had changed," says Bradford. "The first time I heard it, we went to a show in Luton and I said to Susie, 'He's got a problem. He's straining a little bit there.'

"But voices do change over time. It was a natural development. You can't put it down to anything other than when you're working that amount your voice does change. It happens to everybody. If you listen to O'Donnell's first albums and then his later work you'll hear a very different sound."

There are, however, many much older singers who, through careful use, have retained the clear timbre and elasticity of their younger voices. If Dominic's voice -the tool of his trade and the product that the whole mini-industry around him was geared to selling- was suffering from over work, why did he simply not cut down on a schedule that remains as gruelling to this day?

Bradford explains: "I think there's pressures other than Dominic. I wouldn't get too much into the politics of it all, but many times he's told me that he wanted to relax a little bit, and just narrow the whole thing down, which might actually make it more effective.

"But, of course, you've got the record company, you've got management, you've got bands. You've got everything around you. It's a machine that needs to be fed all the time. At the end of the day he could always say, 'No.' But it's not very easy when you're an artist who wants success. When people say, 'We're gonna do this, we're gonna do that, we're gonna put another 35 dates in there...' It's not an easy situation.

"I was always telling him he was doing too much. I've always felt his career should be more structured. Rather than just gig, gig, gig, there should have been a bigger plan behind the whole thing. Just put two solid tours in and the rest of the time promote, which is really what most people do. "We experienced the same thing with Landsborough. I've always found it odd that one week Dominic would be appearing at a major theatre and three weeks later he's doing a working men's club in the same area. That's not part of a structured plan to make a star. And Dominic should have been a major star."

The musical direction of *The Music's Back* was also a departure from Bradford's plan to create a star. Apart from the superb title track, and another enduring favourite from Bradford's pen, *You Are The One,* most of the 14 tracks were familiar covers, including *You're More Than A Number In My Little Red Book, Young Girl* and, with Louise Morrissey playing Dolly Parton to Dominic's Kenny Rogers, *Islands In The Stream.* All were good versions, but none were likely to grab the ear of mainstream DJs who, if they wanted to spin an oldie, could reach for the original.

"My only disappointment is that the record company decided they didn't want it to be so contemporary," says Bradford. "That was their choice entirely. I thought that was a mistake, because we'd built tremendous radio contacts. I think they should have stayed very much in that easy listening, slightly contemporary area. It's midway, really. It's not contemporary and it's not middle of the road. But they decided they wanted to go with a lot more covers. So, fair enough. I said to Mick Clerkin, 'If that's the route you want to go, that's the route we go.' Obviously, we set out to make as good an album as we possibly could."

Promotions man Mike Perry was another who had reservations about the content of *The Music's Back.*

"I think *On The Way To A Dream* was a very progressive album in a way. That's the way he should have gone. I think he should do more contemporary things, really. He then went back and did a covers album and I just think the originals on that album, like *You Are The One* and *The Music's Back* are very strong for Dominic. They go down so well everywhere. I would have gone in that direction. Or, if you're gonna do covers, I'd have done the real big classic covers."

Surprisingly, as he would be the man responsible for selling the music to radio and television, Perry was allowed little input into the song selection.

"I do come into it a little bit, but not as much as I'd like. It's always been pre-ordained by Ritz Records. Clerkin has always had a big control over the music, really. He's always wanted to keep the fan base they've got and never wanted to stray too far. Obviously I'd tell them what feedback I'm getting from radio and what to go with. But, generally, it's Dominic and Clerkin or Eamon Leahy who made the decisions and I think they're afraid of losing that fan base, really.

"It's great to have that concert following, but to have real success I think you have to move on a little bit, and the fans will come with you."

Dominic attributes the direction of *The Music's Back* to Ritz. "I think it was the record company really, because *On The Way To A Dream*, although it did chart for them, they found it more difficult to deal with as in how to get the new songs out and get them to the right people. I think it was a general suggestion that I should look at more covers."

It remains a source of satisfaction to Bradford that his own compositions were the tracks that received the most attention from DJs and fans.

"We only did about two tracks on that album, but luckily the two that got picked up the most were *You Are The One* and *The Music's Back*. I think that's more to do with the fact that they were the original tracks on the album. There were two or three others, but they had been recorded before. They decided to go with *You Are The One* as a single and he got a great reaction to it. It won a radio award and all sorts of things."

With its playful lyrics about the ups and downs of a function band, *The Music's Back* could have been written about

Dominic's early band The Melody Boys. But it wasn't. Nor was it written about Bradford's own background.

"We were in Ireland, I think on a Landsborough tour," says Bradford. "We were talking to Pio McCann, who is a presenter but was a show band artist. He's actually a good friend of Dominic's. I had this song. The melody was right. It was a kind of rock'n'roll thing, but we didn't have a theme for it. So Susie and I were standing in a hotel room having a laugh with Pio and he was talking about the old days. He was going on about, 'Oh, I could have done this but this one left, and he should have done that but his wife got fed up...' And Susie said, 'That's a great idea. That's what this song's got to be all about.' And we turned it into that. She wrote the lyric on that, which I think is a really good lyric. It sums up exactly what the old show band scene was all about."

Dominic immediately identified with the song.

"This is a lot of what Terry's about. He's done his homework about the background you've come from. I suppose there was a certain part of the 1980s and the early 90s where music had gone whatever way it had gone. Discos were a lot more successful and live music wasn't as popular. So Terry wrote this song *The Music's Back* and I was able to adapt to it very quickly. I knew what it was about."

One of the strongest covers on the album was *I Swear*, which had topped the American country charts for John Michael Montgomery and which had also been a pop hit for N'Sync.

"I picked that one," Dominic says proudly. "It's just a very strong song. It's meaningful. As you'll have gathered by now, I'm into lyrics. Lots of people go along with melodies. Melodies are important, but I'm a lyric man and if I hear something that is strong and to the point and I feel there's a message, then that's what I go for. That's what attracted me."

Bradford was happy for Dominic to cut *I Swear*, but it wouldn't have been one of his personal choices.

"He did a very good version of it. In fact, everybody's done it!" Laughs the cockney. "That's one of my big beefs with the whole scene. Once it was a good song, everybody recorded it. It would be far better for the record company if one person recorded it and the attention was focused on that, and everybody got their turn with the good songs. But it never seemed to work like that."

Equally compelling was Dominic's reading of *Love Me Tender,* which Bradford draped in a lush, string arrangement. Twenty years after Elvis Presley's death, it was the first time Dominic had recorded a song associated with his biggest hero. So how did he feel about stepping into the blue suede shoes of The King?

"I didn't think of stepping into Elvis' shoes at all. I wouldn't think like that. I know the popularity of the man throughout the world. Even since his death, people still talk about him and listen to his music. But I would never think I'm gonna do something the exact same way, or I'm gonna sound like Elvis or whatever. That's not what I'm about. I don't do that.

"There's always that argument, why change something that's already a hit?" Dominic reflects. "But Terry had this idea that we should do something different with it and so we did."

On covers generally, Dominic says, "I'd be very careful about trying not to be like other people. When I listen to a track and I like it, I'll listen to it, get the lyrics written out and make sure I know the melody, but that will be the last time I'll ever listen to it. After that, I'll make it mine."

Of the remaining ballads, Dominic was at his most romantic on the soothing *It's All In The Game*, which was embellished with a fine saxophone solo by Chris 'Snake' Davies, and stood up well against high charting versions in the 50s, 60s and 70s by Tommy Edwards, Cliff Richard and the Four Tops, respectively. Gretchen Peters' touching *When You Are Old*, meanwhile, was skilfully chosen to appeal to Dominic's older fans.

Of the uptempo numbers, Dominic found a long-term audience pleaser in his revival of The Drifters' decade old hit, *You're More Than A Number In My Little Red Book*. He was at his most passionate on a faithful cover of Gary Puckett & The Union Gap's 1968 No. 1, *Young* Girl. He also turned in a particularly intense and edgy version of the Searchers' 1964 chart topper *Needles & Pins*, which had been a staple of his shows with The Melody Boys.

"I did it a long time ago when we used to play weddings, but forgot clean about it."

The album was completed by duets with Louise Morrissey who had replaced Tracy Elsdon as Dominic's touring partner. In addition to the revival of *Islands In The Stream* the pair closed the album with the Bradford/Arvesen composition *What More Could I Want From You*. The latter found the dark-haired, elfin-faced Morrissey in fine voice and justified her long-term inclusion on Dominic's tours until she decided to return to her family band in Ireland, The Morrisseys.

"I've great admiration for Louise. I think she's one of the best," says Dominic. "I have worked with different female vocalists on the road and there's something about Louise's voice. Whatever appeal she has to the male side of my audience, she's one of the few females who got a reaction. The other one was Tracy Elsdon. But Louise Morrissey I could see was working with the audience. I feel she's one of the artists that if she got the right breaks she could have a bigger rapport with an audience. I had a good time working with her. We remain friends."

Mindful of the narrow margin by which *On The Way To A Dream* had missed the Top 75 in its week of release, Bradford hatched a strategy to ensure *The Music's Back* fared better. Which it did, entering the national album chart at No. 54.

"I rehearsed Dominic's band for a tour in Ireland. We were probably four months away from the album being released and

I said, 'You will chart if your audience know that it's important to you.'

"That sounds daft, because everyone knows it's important to you. But people don't realise the relevance of when they buy a record and where they buy it. I told Dominic to tell his audience to go out and buy the album in the first week and buy it in the right shops; the big shops."

"He did that on the whole of his tour and I remember a couple of the Ritz people saying, 'What's that crap he's spouting?' But you must never underestimate an audience. People are very loyal. So I just said, 'Chat to every one of your audience at every gig. Say how important it is. Say, 'We missed it by 30 copies, with your help we can do it.' We fashioned a little script for him.

"Now, I'm not saying that's the reason he charted. What I am saying is, it wouldn't have hurt!"

The album was given unexpected TV exposure when Dominic and Louise Morrissey performed *Islands In The Stream* on the BBC's daytime fashion make-over show *Style Challenge*. The producer was an old friend of Mike Perry's, but the promotions man was aided in getting Dominic on the show by fan Moira Clydesdale from Motherwell, who organised a petition of more than 750 signatures to get Dominic on national television. Proudly draped in her Dominic scarf, Moira attended the recording with 150 of her petitioners who formed the most enthusiastic studio audience the show had ever witnessed.

"You must be paying them a lot of money!" Quipped presenter Shauna Lowry as the gathering whooped and hollered at Dominic's arrival, while his wife grinned nervously from the front row.

The premise of the show was to take the raw material of an unshaven Dominic and a make-up free Louise Morrissey and create a dazzling new stage image for each of them. Needless to say, the audience played a noisy part in the decision making process. There were howls of horror as hairdresser Anthony Mascola proposed to comb forward and cut short Dominic's swept back hair for a look "A little bit more rough and ready."

"I think you'd better look for the nearest exit," joked Dominic when the beaming crimper pressed ahead with his plans regardless.

"George Michael started the stubble look," reassured Lowry when Dominic expressed doubts about remaining unshaven. But it was Dominic who got the biggest laugh with the perfectly-timed, straight-faced innocence of "Who's George Michael?"

There were roars of approval when kittenish fashion expert Karen Foster picked out a blue suit with a "Robert DiNiro" style. And, of course, there was plenty of opportunity for innuendo.

"They can't wait to see you get your clothes off!" Grinned Lowry, who clearly couldn't quite believe the strength of Dominic's female following.

"He's going to be performing later... am I allowed to say that!" Blushed make-up artist Mary Vango, who seemed quite weak at the knees from her proximity to the heart throb. She then became the envy of the crowd when, to roars of delight, she unbuttoned the singer's shirt to reveal a thickly-haired chest and give him a relaxing neck massage. Dominic, who had looked decidedly uncomfortable while Mascola snipped off his locks, looked the happiest he'd been during the show.

And the result of the thirty minute make-over?

When they came out to close the show with *Islands In The Stream*, an immaculately made up Louise Morrissey looked stunned by her new outfit of shiny black trousers and shiny, skimpy boob tube worn under a black jacket. But Dominic looked as pleased as punch in a roomy Identikit blue suit, black v-neck t-shirt and black suede shoes, his newly cropped hair offset by a trendy designer stubble.

"He didn't keep the hairstyle too long, but I thought it made him look a lot younger, " comments Mike Perry.

"I may go back to it, you never know. There's photographs of me at home with that hairstyle." Of his appearance on the show, generally, he says, "It was a good day's fun. It was another form of getting to national media, which is what it was really all about. It wasn't so much about getting a new hairstyle or anything. I think Louise Morrissey enjoyed it but, like myself, she wasn't totally happy with the final result. But it was all fun."

The darkened and swept forward hair looked particularly sharp coupled with a black suit when Dominic made a return appearance on the Art Sutter show. Looking seriously cool, and the most contemporary he had ever looked on the small screen, the singer lappeared like a man at the top of his profession as he grooved through the engaging *You're More Than A Number In My Little Red Book*. He got to say as much in a brief chat with the host that allowed him to demonstrate the conversational skill of the smoothest politician in keeping the talk 'on message.'

Sutter began by asking Dominic about his vocal problems and, with the merest nod of acknowledgement, the singer swept the conversation away from such negative matters to the far more important news that *The Music's Back* had just entered the pop charts at number 54. Naturally there were plenty of fans in the audience to raise the roof in response and, to their loudly expressed delight, the singer accepted Sutter's invitation to stand up, unbutton his jacket and reprise one of his famous hip gyrations. In every way it was a performance that proved Dominic was now completely at home in front of the TV cameras, both as a singer and personality.

Attesting to Dominic's rising profile in the entertainment industry, the singer also began to find himself on the guest list of various celebrity functions. A party for Ulster TV's *Kelly Live* show found Dominic hob-nobbing with snooker stars Dennis

Taylor and John Parrot, comedian Jimmy Cricket and various actors from the cast of *Coronation Street* on the set of TV's most famous pub, The Rovers Return. Dominic sang *Northern Lights Are Shining For Me* on the broadcast part of the evening.

Dominic also participated alongside Cliff Richard at Radio Clyde's 'Cash For Kids' charity fundraiser.

On The Way To A Dream entered the pop charts at number 76. *The Music's Back* went in at number 54. Terry Bradford was certain that his next album with Dominic would do even better. But although Bradford was booked to produce a third Kirwan album, a last-minute decision was taken to record Dominic's next CD across the Atlantic in Nashville.

"Everyone needs to get a Nashville album out of their system," says Dominic's earlier producer Shaun Wallace. Bradford takes a similar view.

Recognising the kudos of a Nashville produced album in the British country market, Bradford readily concedes his own recording set up is "Not glamorous by any stretch." Neither was Bradford unduly upset at being dropped as Dominic's producer.

"Of course, I wasn't too pleased. But that's the way they make their decisions and good luck to them. I've been in the business a long time and you don't have exclusivity with anyone. I think other people might have thought I was more upset than I actually was."

Artistically, however, Bradford believes that taking Dominic's recording operation to Nashville was "A silly move."

"I know the Nashville album sold a lot, so that would be fine with the record company. I think. I don't know. By that time the record company had changed dramatically. The expectations may have changed as well. But I know the Nashville album didn't chart, so I find that disappointing.

"Our plan was to go upwards, which is what we did. We started off at 76. The next one was 54. That's in a short period.

I felt that we were working to a plan to create a national star. Not in the market that he's involved in. I always felt everybody was too content just to keep his market satisfied and weren't too interested about bringing more people in.

"I always thought Dominic should go into Europe. But there was a bit of reluctance to let anybody have any sort of control over the artists. They did licence albums to Australia and, to a certain extent, America. But they had their own company represented in Australia, so they weren't really giving away any control.

"Dominic's album *On The Way To A Dream* could have very easily gone into Holland, into Scandinavian countries and all sorts. And there would have been a lot of people who would have picked that up. We had contacts to suggest. We didn't do anything, because that wasn't our place. But there were contacts with whom we could at least have started dialogue in those territories. But it was never looked at by Ritz."

What would a third Terry Bradford studio project have been like?

"I would have tried to make it a little bit more contemporary again. You can obviously record a song that you know is going to appeal to his audience, but I think this business has got to go further than the existing people. I don't mean that you will alienate that audience, because they're the people that made Dominic what he is. So you've got to please those. But that doesn't mean you can't try and please a few other people as well. If you can do that then your market's growing."

Maybe that third Bradford-produced album will one day become a reality.

"My experience of Terry has been good and maybe I'll work with him again," says Dominic. "In fact I probably will. In the back of my mind I feel I will, at some stage, do something." ■

CHAPTER TEN

The Town I Love so Well

THE M1 DOM number plate and maroon metallic nose of the Shogun is splattered with the streaked remains of flies, silent testament to the motorway miles the vehicle has put in during a couple of weeks that have taken it from Bournemouth to Wales, to Birmingham, to Scotland and to the Orkney Islands. Today it's parked by the stage door of the Corn Exchange in King's Lynn. The backdrop is a sprawling car park, simmering under a rare May heat haze and, beyond that, the watery expanse of The Wash. The sun is shining. It's a day not unlike the one three years before that changed forever Dominic's hometown.

Saturday the 15th of August, 1998 was a typically busy day in Omagh. With two weeks to go before school resumed, the town centre was particularly full of families shopping for school uniforms in S.D. Kells and Watersons. A carnival was due later in the day.

Amid the general bustle nobody paid any attention to the maroon Vauxhall Cavalier driven to Market Street and parked outside Kells' clothes store, or to the two male occupants who walked quietly away down Campsie Road. None of the busy shoppers passing by could have known that the car had been stolen the previous Thursday. Or that it contained 300 pounds of fertiliser-based explosive with a Semtex trigger.

Half an hour after the car was parked, Ulster Television in Belfast received a 30-minute bomb warning. The warning specified the Courthouse, 500 yards away, as the target. The police immediately cordoned off the named area and began moving people towards the supposed safety of Market Street. In doing so they inadvertently doubled the number of people in the vicinity when the bomb went off at ten minutes past three.

Twenty one people died instantly. More than two hundred others suffered burns, lost limbs, were hit by flying glass and masonry or were deafened by the explosion. The eventual death toll would be 29 plus unborn twins.

The entire front wall of Kells was blasted back into the building, causing the roof to collapse on to the first floor. The furniture of the nearby Pine Emporium was blown through the shop and could later be seen sticking out of the rear windows. Adding to the hellish scene, a water main exposed by the blast began gushing and washing bodies down the hill.

In the King's Lynn dressing room almost three years later, Dominic is wearing an untucked, pale blue short-sleeved shirt. He's playing mum, today. For once, Ali is not in attendance. Dominic's son, Colm, is in the UK for an audition at the Guildford School Of Music and Ali has volunteered to chauffeur him from the airport. Left to fend for himself, Dominic is coping -just. Having tracked down a bottle of water in the bathroom, he rummages in his bag for a tube of shrink-wrapped plastic tumblers. He prises the first one out and discovers it's been cracked in transit. The second one has suffered similarly. Eventually, Dominic realises that they are all cracked but, luckily, only halfway down their length.

"It'll be all right if you drink from that side and I only fill it up to there," he says, pulling up a chair beside the dressing table. The much-needed refreshments attended to, Dominic turns his mind back to the day of the bomb.

It's hot in the dressing room, and the window is open. It only looks out on to a narrow alley and a blank brick wall, but the sun is still shining in. Dominic gestures towards it.

"I remember it well," he says, "It was a day like that there. It was a lovely afternoon."

Dominic was at home, with family friends the Guirys as his guests.

"Peter was at the house that day as well. He'd called round that afternoon. The lady of the family, Nell Guiry, wanted to get her hair done and through my wife, Louise, they'd organised an appointment with a hairdresser who was at the far end of the town. Peter was going in that direction, because it was his side of the town, so he had left the house and taken my guest with him.

"My kids, thank God, were all at home that day. That was funny, because it was Saturday afternoon and teenage boys usually like to meet with their friends on a Saturday. But they didn't. So, we were in the kitchen, maybe having a cup of coffee or whatever. We heard nothing. But one of the boys, it may have been Barry, came into the kitchen and said he heard a thud. that sounded like a bomb but being in the kitchen on that side of the house we didn't hear anything.

"Then, maybe five minutes after that, Peter phoned me and said, 'Did you hear that?' 'Hear what?' So he explained the story that they were driving along, not that far from the bomb area, and he felt that some guy had driven into the back of him. That's how it felt to him. That's how close he was. He said, 'There's a bomb. There's a bomb gone off in the town.'"

"Everyone was in confusion, because nobody knew at the time who was where. It was then that I got in the vehicle and thought, well, I'll go and see what's happening or maybe what I could do.

"In Northern Ireland, if a bomb goes off, some people would go and check out what it was. Other people would say, 'It's not the place for me to be.' I'm that type of guy. So I didn't jump immediately when I heard it was a bomb. You immediately think to yourself, 'I hope everybody's OK. That they got everybody out.' And in most cases they do. Because the area will be cleared.

"But we got a call not long after to say this looks like a bad one. So, like everybody else, I jumped in my vehicle. But, by that stage, the town was completely cordoned off. There was absolutely no way of getting in.

"Not long after that, you'd switch on the radio or the television, because you'd know there were going to be fatalities. Word gets out very fast. But it was worse than that The television then immediately started requesting for doctors and nurses to report back to duty. We then knew that things weren't good."

McGlone in the meantime, had met a friend whose daughter was unaccounted for. They'd headed to the town centre and, fortunately, met the daughter running injured from the scene.

"They drove her to the hospital," says Dominic, "and when they got there he said it was like something you'd see in Beirut. There were people laying everywhere. There was blood everywhere. There were no beds. The hospital was totally stretched out.

"They were doing the best they could and, obviously, trying to get the main injuries sorted. Army helicopters were being used to ship people off to other hospitals."

It was, quite simply, Northern Ireland's largest ever medical emergency operation.

Like many people, Dominic was initially unsure how to respond to the tragedy.

"The town was thrown into a complete turmoil. For me, it was confusing. You knew this was major. Now, you can look back and think maybe we could have helped in some way. I don't know why, but we didn't. But there were many people who did. With teas and coffees through the night, comforting people who couldn't account for their loved ones."

Dominic looks thoughtfully for a moment at the hands resting on his crossed knee. He takes a deep breath.

"It was within a few days that I realised the part I could do. It was to go on the road. We were starting a tour on the Wednesday, more or less the first day of the funerals. So, it was to go on the road and make people aware of, well, 'Things are moving on. There is a fund there if anyone would like to help.' And that's what we did. And, along the way, I think we raised something in the region of £30,000."

A large sun was raised at a single benefit gig at the Galtymore club in London, organised by Dominic's old friend from The Melody Boys, Barry Bradley.

Based in London since the early 80s, Bradley had been visiting his home town immediately prior to the bombing.

"I'd left Omagh on that day to travel back to London, so it felt very close," says Bradley, who now heads his own band, The Breeze. "That and the fact that I have a niece, Nicola Bradley, who was injured in the bombing. That kinda brought it home.

"I've always stayed in touch with Dominic. He's often got up and sung with my band when he's in town. In fact he's Godfather to one of my daughters. So, a few weeks, or maybe a month after, Dominic was in town. I had it on my mind, so I said to Dominic, 'Is there any chance we could get a date together and maybe do something?' That fell into place lovely. And there were other people from Omagh who live in London that helped out a lot as well."

"Total credit to the man," says Dominic. "I suppose we helped the situation. But Barry did the work. He did the homework. And we raised something like £11,000 in one night."

"It was a great night and very emotional," says Bradley. "There were quite a few other bands from London. Seamus Moore, who was one of the first people to put us up when The Melody Boys first came to London was there, and a few others. It was very well supported. Surprisingly, for a Monday night. Lot's of people put up different prizes for the raffle and I think it was Ritz that put up a gold disc, made up for the night, which Dominic signed. They auctioned it for £3000. I don't think it was so much what it was. It was just that people were so generous. They wanted to help."

Living in a community of just 25,000 souls, it would have been difficult not to be affected on some personal level by an atrocity as large as the one that struck Omagh, especially for a member of the community as well known as Dominic.

"We learned very soon who was killed, and we knew many of the people," Dominic says quietly. "We might not have known all the people who lost their lives, but we knew many of the families.

"One of the lasting memories for me was visiting homes and wakes.

"You started in the afternoon and you were still going at twelve o'clock at night, going from house to house. You would go from one house to the next and you'd be coming out of the door and speaking to the same people that were at the last house. Everybody was just passing their last respects to the families. I don't think I'll ever forget that.

Then, of course, there were the more personal memories. A week previous, on a Saturday night, I had a night off. I was out with my wife and some friends. We went into a local bar, Broderick's, which I would use when I have nights off because it's a place where you can sit and talk with people. There's no music there. I mean, as much as I love music, when I go out for the night I like to go to where you can chat.

"That particular night we were sitting in the front bar. It's not a big bar, so we could hear a lot of hullabaloo coming from the back. There was a lot of giggling and gaggling going on, and it soon became obvious there were a group of ladies out enjoying themselves. It was a hen party for a girl who I'd known and grown up with in Centenary Park, Mary McGinn who's now Mary McCullough. Although physically handicapped for most of her life, she has never been one to let her handicap get in the way of her enjoyment. She was getting married within two weeks. All her female friends were out for the night and they were going next door to the local dance hall. They had to pass me on the way out and I knew them all. I'd known them from growing up in the town together. We were having a bit of a laugh and a bit of a chat. I wouldn't see them that often. Of course, the cameras were flying on the night. There were photographs taken with me and it was great to see them all. One girl in particular was called Geraldine Breslin. I've known Geraldine, God, most of my life."

Dominic pauses, before adding quietly, "Geraldine lost her life in the bomb."

The Omagh bombing was not the first time Dominic had been closely affected by the Troubles. Two years previous, the truck carrying his equipment was being driven home after a show when it was flagged down by three masked terrorists, hijacked and burned by the roadside.

"We'd done a festival in South Armagh," says Dominic. "It was a good night. It was a very good night, in fact. I had stopped back afterwards to meet the audience, as I do. In most cases, I'm generally away before the road crew. But on this occasion I wasn't. I'd stayed back and met the committee and had a drink with them, and got paid. We headed back towards home and, as we were approaching the city of Armagh we could see in the distance flashing lights.

"We rounded a corner and I knew, immediately, that it was our truck because, at that time, my name was on the side of it. It was well alight.

"As I got out of the vehicle, one of the firemen spotted me. He said, 'Where are your drivers? Where are your crew?' I looked at the cab and at that stage it was totally gutted. By that stage the fire had moved to the back of the truck. So, for the next forty minutes or so it wasn't a nice time. Nobody knew where they were.

"We were later to find out that they had been hijacked by a couple of guys in masks. They had been ordered to go in one direction and the hijackers had jumped in the truck and gone in the other. Apparently, it was hilarious in many ways. From what I believe, they didn't even know how to drive the truck. They were crashing the gears. But they were just out to get a vehicle that night. They crossed the road and set it alight blocking the road."

"But the fire tender was there within twenty minutes. They radioed ahead to the police and the next thing we heard was that the crew had arrived at the local police station to report the hijacking. So, thankfully, nobody was injured.

"We lost everything," Dominic says solemnly. "We lost everything.

"The funny thing about the stuff was it was more or less me leaving school at 16 years of age, getting in bands, and building, building, building up to that stage. That was what was in the back of that truck. My life was in the back of that truck. My business was in the back of that truck. So, we lost the business over night, really."

"Dominic said he cried when he saw it," recalls Jim McLarnon, at his home near Manchester. "Everything he had, all his equipment and everything else had gone up in smoke."

"Again, I have to be more than grateful to my sponsor, Jim McLarnon,. We hired equipment from one of the hire companies in Northern Ireland, then Jim helped me to purchase the equipment we've had for the last couple of years."

Jim adds: "When Dominic phoned me at five o'clock in the

morning, he was crying. But we rallied round and he was back on the road by just after dinner the next day."

In retrospect, Dominic says, "I think we probably came back on the road too fast. Charlie, my manager at the time felt there were shows to be done and we were committed. But we really didn't take the shock on board."

In the aftermath of the hijacking, Dominic says, "Obviously, the case was taken up by the Northern Ireland Office. But I didn't get everything that was lost, unfortunately. There was a shortfall of about £20,000 that has never been recouped. The members of the band at the time did better out of it than I did, because they all got new equipment and, in some cases, maybe better equipment than what they'd had.

"Now, when I look back at it, I think we were given the wrong information by our solicitors. Every man should have had his own personal claim. But we brought it in under one claim. So, whatever the short fall was in the end, muggins here took the fall."

As for the question of who was responsible for the hijacking, Dominic prefers not to dwell on the matter.

"I believe it was a case of being in the wrong place at the wrong time. Northern Ireland at that time was very heated. It was the first year of what we know as the Drumcree situation. The country was very much at boiling point.

"I have never, over the years, let that get in my way as far as where I want to go and where I wanted to work. All aspects of the Northern Ireland community have been good to me. I don't see religion as a barrier. People throughout the world may see the religious situation in Northern Ireland like that, but I totally disbelieve that. It may have been like that many years ago, but definitely not over these last few years. I've never seen religion as a barrier. I see good on all sides of the community and, hence, I'm willing to work wherever people are willing to have me.

"The local television obviously wanted me to talk, but I wouldn't get involved in that because I knew in my heart I wasn't involved in anything. For me to go on television and say who I thought did this would be totally ridiculous. I suppose there are some people who are good at using the media for their own purposes in these situations, but I didn't go that way."

One of the saddest aspects of the troubles in Northern Ireland is the readiness for cruel pranksters to perpetuate the fear and anguish generated by the various atrocities. Since the August 1998 bomb, Omagh town centre has been regularly brought to a standstill by hoax bomb warnings. Dominic was the victim of a similar hoax shortly after the hijacking.

"I think it was a couple of nights after we got back on the road that we were doing a show in Dungannon and there was a bomb scare. The police felt it had been linked to the incident a few nights previous. But they said, 'Look, if you're happy to go on with the show we'll go with it.'" With a chuckle, Dominic adds, "So we did the show. Then we got a police escort to the border. So it was quite funny.

"We also had a bomb scare one night at the Corn Exchange in Cambridge. I remember Scotland Yard coming on to the scene. I think if it had been more localised police they would have dealt with it at the time. But because the call had come through Scotland Yard they were not happy to let it sit. So they wouldn't let us on with the show on the night."

Having been so close to such incidents as the hijacking and the Omagh bomb, not to mention the countless other bombs, shootings and violence that, for many years, had made Northern Ireland an almost permanent fixture on the nation's news, had Dominic, who had greater resources and opportunities than many of his countrymen, ever considered moving his family to the safer environment of the mainland?

"The troubles in Northern Ireland would never have made me move. Never," the singer says firmly. "If anything had made me move, it would have been my business. But, I've said in many interviews that I don't live that far from my work. It takes me three hours by car to travel to Dublin and I can be anywhere in the UK in three hours. So I think Omagh is as good a place to live as anywhere in the UK. It's done me no wrong.

"I don't know if everybody would agree with me but it really isn't a bad, bigoted town. If anything, it is a town that should be taken seriously about how people are living, and how they can live.

"Omagh has got a serious amount to offer. It's got good schools. It's got leisure facilities. It probably needs a little bit more industry and it's not that far away from airports and boats.

"One of the saddest things today is the hospital situation. I think Omagh, down through the years, was always renowned for having a good hospital. But, as in many parts of the UK, they've been streamlined. And yet, on that particular day, if we hadn't had that local hospital, I would hate to think what the fatalities would have been.

"If it's only as a lasting memory to the troubles of Northern Ireland, I believe Omagh should have a major hospital. It needs something major. From that day we've had prime ministers, we've had presidents in our town. And it's been great for the people to have all that. But the real question is what are they really doing? That hasn't been seen yet.

"But, as for moving away from Omagh, I have no intention of doing that." ■

CHAPTER ELEVEN

Wish You Were Here

IN 1996, Dominic's music reached a new market, 12,000 miles away on the other side of the world. It's an experience he will never forget.

"I remember being put up in the Regency Hotel in Sydney which looked right across the bay. I arrivedaround five in the morning and remember looking out and seeing the sun rise over Sydney. From my bedroom window you could see the harbour, the bay, the opera house. It was like looking at a picture post card. I was like touching myself and thinking, 'Hold on, is this really real?'

"I remember making phone calls home and telling them, 'I'm sitting looking over the harbour and you wouldn't believe it, this is a sight for sore eyes.' The sun was just coming up and I was on the other end of the world."

Dominic's first visit to Australia came from a licensing deal between Ritz and Australian outlet Massive Records. Laurie Dunn, the founder of Massive, first travelled to the UK, like so many of his young countrymen, as a tanned and enthusiastic back-packer on a working holiday. He landed a job working for Richard Branson at Virgin Records in London and eventually returned home as managing director of Virgin (Australia).

When Virgin became interested in Daniel O'Donnell for the Australian market, Laurie returned to London to sign a distribution deal for his territory. Dunn's first call was to publicist Tony Byworth.

A rare Englishman in the Ritz camp, Byworth had been involved in the British country music scene in various capacities since 1969 when he was one of the founders of the British Country Music Association. A self-confessed Jack of all trades, Byworth moved into journalism, writing about country music in *Billboard* and *Record Mirror* before taking over editorship of the UK's longest running country magazine, *Country Music People*. After several years in that role, Byworth started an independent press relations company which, over time, has seen him represent in the UK most American country singers from Crystal Gayle to Garth Brooks. Byworth was a natural choice to handle publicity for Ritz and, because of his many contacts in Nashville, quickly proved useful to the company in a wider role. At one point he became a director, alongside Mick Clerkin, of Ritz America, a subsidiary formed to handle Ritz recording and touring activities across the Atlantic.

Of the tie-up between Ritz and Massive, which resulted in the formation of a new imprint, Ritz Records Australia, Byworth recalls: "A deal was agreed, then EMI bought Virgin – and Laurie left the company. It could have been an awkward situation, dealing with a label that no longer had the person on board that had signed the act, and who were possibly not interested in the act, but things worked out as Laurie then launched his own independent label, Massive, and we managed to get Daniel off Virgin and on to Massive. It was a case of 'better the person you know.' To help get Massive off the ground, I put Laurie in touch with Charley Pride, who is a huge star in Australia and New Zealand, and a deal was struck with him for that territory."

With O'Donnell quickly established as a major draw in the Antipodes, Dominic was clearly the next in line to follow him. The compilation *Introducing Dominic Kirwan* whetted Australian appetites for Ireland's most dynamic entertainer and received good radio exposure. The catalyst for his first promotional trip, however, was the lucky decision by the Fred Hollows Foundation to use Dominic's track *We'll Be Together From Now On* as the theme for its 1996 fund-raising campaign.

The song was written by producer Bradford and his partner Susie Arvesen and originally appeared on the album *On The Way To A Dream*. Of the song's creation, Bradford recalls, "I've always been an audience watcher, whether you're on stage looking out, whether you're standing behind someone as a musical director, or whether you're in the audience. And that song was very attached to Dominic's audience.

"One of the things we wanted to do was write a song that, first and foremost, in the oldest sense of the word, would get people tapping their feet. And we wanted to write a love song, but not a straightforward, bog standard love song. Susie came up with the idea of the lyric and the idea was that he would perform that song to his audience. You know what his audience is like. They're incredibly devoted, and the idea of the lyric is it's more about him and his audience than anything else. So it was a semi-love song but more one he could perform directly to that audience."

"Someone from the Fred Hollows Foundation heard this song on their car radio and applied the words in a completely different way. It just shows how different people can interpret a piece of music."

The Fred Hollows Foundation is a charity fighting blindness in Australia's Aboriginal community and other deprived areas of the world. Approached by the Foundation's executive who had heard Dominic's song on the radio, Laurie Dunn struck a deal whereby 50 cents was donated to the charity from every copy of *We'll Be Together From Now On* that was sold, and the single was shipped to 160 radio stations across the country.

"That was dead lucky," recalls Byworth. "It was very beneficial because their campaign went on throughout the year and they were using Dominic's song all the time. I believe the single sold pretty well. It certainly got a lot of attention."

It wasn't the first or last time that a singer has benefited from association with a prominent charity campaign. But as well as giving Dominic some unexpected exposure, the tie-in also served the Fred Hollows Foundation well. True to his generous and conscientious nature Dominic worked hard to promote the cause at every opportunity during his short visit. In fact, the eloquent Irishman proved to be a perfect ambassador for the charity.

Although Hollows is a name little known outside of Australia, where the late ophthalmologist is remembered as a local hero, Dominic took time to find out about the man and the Foundation that bore his name.

"He was from New Zealand and a quite remarkable man. . . in fact, a rebel," explained Dominic during one of his many interviews during the trip. "He developed a lens that could be implanted in the cataract of the eye and restore sight. At first the cost of manufacturing these lenses was incredibly high but Fred Hollows was able to put them into mass production at specially built plants and bring the cost down to a few dollars a lens."

Even Hollows' widow, Gabi, and her associates were impressed by Dominic's knowledge of her husband and the Foundation's work when he lunched with them after singing *We'll Be Together From Now On* for a nationwide television audience on Channel 9's *Midday With Kerri-Anne* show within a couple of days of stepping from the plane.

"I read up on it before coming out to Australia. Quite honestly I wanted to make sure that I knew about the charity and what the record was representing. There's nothing worse than to be uninformed about a situation."

The April 96 visit was designed as a short but intensive schedule of press, radio and television interviews, along with a handful of small scale singing appearances.

Clerkin and Byworth were due to accompany Dominic but on the morning of their evening flight from London, Byworth answered his phone to hear a familiar Irish voice: "I don't think I'll be going. You go and look after Dominic yourself."

"Mick didn't want to travel around, but I was happy to go with Dominic and see Australia," says Byworth. By the end of the trip, however, he understood why Clerkin had decided to give the whirlwind visit a miss.

"I don't know how guys like Dominic do it all the time," sighs Tony, still sounding tired five years later. A glance at the schedule drawn up by Laurie Dunn tells its own exhausting story:

April 10 -John Laws Show (Radio 2UE), Midday Show (Channel 9), fly to Melbourne.

April 11 -Good Morning Australia (Channel 9), fly to Hobart, Tasmania for guest appearance at Mary From Dungloe Ball and perform five or six songs.

April 12 -Fly to Melbourne for performance on Hey Hey It's Saturday (Channel 9) and perform at Melbourne Mary From Dungloe Ball.

April 13 -Fly back to Sydney to perform at the Sydney Mary From Dungloe Ball. . .

In all, Dominic did more than twenty interviews in ten days with some 'phoners' to live radio shows undertaken even before he'd had his usual breakfast of fresh fruit, muesli and coffee. During the little downtime available, he even squeezed in a little sightseeing including a ferry ride across Sydney Harbour and a trip to the zoo where a koala bear was the only Australian to display an ockerish indifference to the visiting star. Dominic tickled his head and the animal messed on his shirt.

Naturally, in addition to the Fred Hollows connection, Dominic's first trip to Australia also targeted the Irish community.

"The thing with Dominic and Daniel is that there's always an Irish audience somewhere," explains Byworth. "The Irish are very loyal. It's like, 'He's one of us so we'll go and see him.' As we did in England, you start with that audience and expand from there."

Despite years of working with Ritz, Byworth was tickled once more by the extent to which the Irish connection worked on a personal level.

"It's like the Irish are linked up all over the world. Everywhere they go there are people who know them, or at least know of them, or know somebody who knows them, if they don't know them personally. I remember on the flight down to Sydney, Dominic and myself both like aisle seats and we had seats on opposite sides of the aisle. He sat down and straight away sitting beside him was a lady who knew him!

"It was funny because wherever we went on the promo visit there was always some Irish person ready to take us out for a drink or a meal. I became a sort of honorary Irishman. The alien Irishman."

The Irish fans were out in force when Dominic flew to the Tasmanian capital of Hobart, a picturesque harbour town with shades of the Cornish coast, to guest at the Mary From Dungloe Ball. The celebrations were staged at the Laetare Gardens and Dominic's dinner stretched over a couple of hours as he tried to swallow the occasional mouthful between signing autographs for the four hundred strong crowd.

The Mary From Dungloe Balls are one of the most important events on the Irish calendar. The tradition is based on the legend of Mary Gallagher from Dungloe on the coast of Donegal. When her parents disapproved of her relationship with a local lad, he emigrated to America and she was forced to move with her family to New Zealand, never to see her lover again.

The story was told in a poem which was later put to music and recorded by Emmett Spiceland who had a huge Irish hit with the number in 1967. Soon after, the Mary From Dungloe Balls were set up as a pageant-cum-beauty contest in which Irish girls around the world compete to win a holiday in Ireland.

Following in the footsteps of Daniel O'Donnell, who had hosted several of the regional festivals on his tour of Australia the previous year, Dominic happily agreed to preside over balls in Hobart, Melbourne and Sydney. After all, who was better qualified to serenade the winning 'Marys' than Ireland's Number One heart throb?

It was an Australian admirer, Val Green, writing on an internet fansite, who bestowed the title 'No Greater Gyrator' on Dominic, and he lived up to the description not just during a seven-song set backed by local group The Cockies, but when he demonstrated his prize-winning footwork by joining in with a troupe of traditional Irish dancers.

Compared with the rural setting of Hobart, the Balls at the Celtic Club, Melbourne and the Bankstown Sports Club, on the outskirts of Sydney, were more formal affairs. Indeed, the black tie guest list in Sydney was headed by Irish Ambassador to Australia Richard O'Brien and his wife. Drawing from the more densely populated urban areas, the Irish contingent in Melbourne and Sydney was even stronger than in Hobart, and although he had little time to rehearse with his backing musicians, they raised the roof when Dominic sang his fund-raising song *We'll Be Together From Now On* and, particularly, when he sang the traditional *Mary From Dungloe* to the winning contestants Gabriele McGabe and Stephanie Jupp.

As the man himself put it, "The evenings were great. But serenading the ladies was an unexpected pleasure."

It was intended that Dominic's highly successful promotional visit would pave the way for an Australian tour that would swiftly follow. In the event, almost three years elapsed before Dominic returned to the Sunburnt Land. Laurie Dunn wanted Dominic in Australia to promote his records. Dominic and publicist Tony Byworth both felt the need to capitalise as soon as possible on the awareness they had created with the media trip. Ritz, however, felt that Dominic's energies would be better spent at home.

"The politics at Ritz had changed from my previous years working at the company. It had become a plc. A new guy, Paddy Prendagrast, moved in as CEO and Clerkin had less say in day-to-day activities," says Byworth.

In the end, Dominic, Dunn and Byworth organised his first Australian concert tour themselves without the support of Ritz. With thirteen near sell-out dates all over Australia and New Zealand, it was an incredible achievement, especially as Dominic insisted on giving his Australian fans exactly the same show he performed in the UK, which meant taking his full band and sound and lighting crew with him.

Of the lack of involvement by Ritz, Dominic reflects, "Ritz is a record company and people must remember that. They're not a management company. Like any other record company, I suppose, they'll get your product out, but it's really up to you to sort something out with it.

"I suppose the record company was happy to put one or two people on a flight, but when it came to taking the whole band nobody wanted to cover it."

Despite his pragmatism, it's clear Dominic was hurt by the lack of support.

"I suppose within myself I thought that I wasn't given a lot of faith by the record company that I could do anything. So it was nice when we were able to prove that we could do something and, with the help of Laurie down there, we did business. The tour itself may not have been totally financially viable, but we must remember that it was a first time operation. The tour was successful. We sold a lot of product and we created an interest."

Of setting up the tour, Byworth recalls: "I first approached Arthur Laing, who is the manager/booker for the legendary Australian singer Slim Dusty. On that first promo tour I'd wanted to meet Arthur as much as anything because I'd just worked with Slim when he visited the UK. I thought maybe Arthur could book Dominic some dates. We had a good meeting and he said he'd look into it, but nothing happened. I followed it up for a year, but we were getting nowhere."

Enter Australian country singer and journalist Keith Glass, who was supplementing his income as a club-land entertainer by helping with the promotional aspects of Massive Records.

"Keith was working out of Laurie's office," Byworth continues, "So I said to Laurie one day, 'Keith knows the clubs, can't he do the bookings?' And before we knew it, he got these dates together."

Says Keith Glass: "By that stage the Ritz name was synonymous with acts that could draw a core audience, spearheaded by the incredible success of Daniel O'Donnell. While Dominic was nowhere as well known, it was thought that he would at least have a bottom line crowd to draw on and the on-stage ability to make a major impression.

"One problem was the time of year available. February is not the best time to tour an act such as Dominic. The main audience is middle-aged and they are still in recovery from the long Christmas/New Year holidays in Australia, as it is high summer. However, it was the time Dominic and his band could come, given their busy schedule, so we set to it. Put in place was a two-and-a-half week tour taking in the South-East Coast of Australia and the island state of Tasmania; the main population base that could be effectively covered by road and air at a realistic price given the size of the touring party. Advance sales in most areas were encouraging, with a very loyal Ritz core group giving an early boost."

Without the backing of Ritz, however, there remained the question of who was going to finance Dominic's Australian tour.

"Hopefully we were going to break even," says Byworth, "but, first time around, tours generally lose money. Unless we had someone to underwrite it we were fixed. Laurie was going to pay for record promotion, but he wasn't going to underwrite air fares from Britain -and Dominic wanted to take the whole band over. That's a lot of people. Laurie and me both suggested to Dominic that he took a cut-down band and augmented it with some Australian musicians. But Dominic insisted that he wanted to do the show he would normally do over here. Which was fair enough, but the economics didn't make sense.

"We were stuck with this situation. The tour was going over there and who was going to pay for it? We weren't getting anywhere with Ritz, who were against the idea. Keith was getting concerned, having booked the dates, and we were still not certain we were going."

The day was saved once more by Dominic's sponsors Jim and Kath McLarnon of Stamford Van & Car Hire, who were happy to help out their friend by once more digging into their deep pockets, this time for the hardly trifling price of 16 return flights to the other side of the world, plus all the internal flights around Australia. Dominic didn't even have to ask for the money.

"Because they'd been interested in my life and my career there would have been many things talked about in their home," says Dominic. "Jim's a guy that sits and listens, and he never speaks that often about certain things. But he knew that I wanted to go to Australia and that it was what I felt should be done. The record company were not being very forthcoming and Jim said, 'If you can see a way to get this up and running, I'll do what I can to cover the expenses of the flights."

As usual with the McLarnons' sponsorship of Dominic, business considerations were not part of the deal. "It was pure loving of the lad," says Kath. "Ritz was flaffing about. He was going, he wasn't going. So at the end of the day my husband said, 'Oh go. I'll help you."

Responding to the suggestion that the cost of sending 16 people to Australia was a lot of money to spend out of love, Jim replies with a self-deprecating chuckle, "I suppose to some people it probably would be."

But it certainly wasn't money he was afraid of losing. Asked if he got his money back from the venture, Jim says simply, "I didn't want the money back. The money that Kath and I put in was for the love of Dominic. We didn't want our money back on that."

Neither did McLarnon question Dominic's wishes to take his full band and crew with him.

"We left nobody out," says Jim. "We said from the beginning that we wouldn't leave anybody out. It wouldn't be fair to any member of the crew to say, 'Sorry, we can't afford to take you,' and we didn't want to cause any resentment because somebody couldn't go."

The project, however, was not quite out of the woods. Less than a week before embarkation, Laurie Dunn received a worrying fax from Tony Byworth Associates.

Dear Laurie,

Well I don't know how much problem this will be, but Dominic and crew don't have visas for New Zealand. When I spoke to him this morning he said he hadn't done anything about it and it wasn't on the list of 'things to be done' sent to him by Keith Glass a few weeks back. . .

It was potentially disastrous, at least for the first two dates on the tour, due to begin in the New Zealand town of Dunedin. Dominic was on the road with gigs scheduled until the Sunday of departure. There was no way he'd be able to sort out the matter of work permits for himself, his band and crew.

Fortunately for those in the music business, bureaucracy has a way of dissolving a lot quicker than it tends to for the general public. But not without a lot of work behind the scenes.

Recalling a frantic 24 hours cutting through red tape, Byworth explains: "Laurie found someone in the New Zealand High Commission in London. I called him up and he gave me the name of a New Zealand representative in Dublin who got the necessary visas together (after speaking to the promoter in New Zealand who confirmed that he was putting on the dates and that Dominic and band would be leaving the country after the shows) and one of Dominic's crew travelled to Dublin to pick up the visas."

With that final hurdle cleared, Dominic boarded a plane for his second 23 hour flight Down Under.

The first show at Dunedin Town Hall in New Zealand was a complete success. But the evening was marred by news of a terrible tragedy.

Dominic's manager, Charlie McBrien had stayed home in Ireland. He had given the Australian visit his blessing but had not been involved in it, preferring like Ritz to concentrate his efforts on his home market.

"Charlie was a very nice guy," recalls Byworth, "he was really a good old Irish fella. But his interest as far as Dominic was concerned, was Ireland. UK dates were booked out of Ritz, because Ritz at that time had their own touring department, and they would do the tour bookings in the UK. Charlie's area, what he knew, was Ireland."

Digressing, Byworth recalls: "One of the craziest experiences with Charlie occurred in Belfast with Crystal Gayle when we needed to get to Dublin. Charlie volunteered to drive us and he was like a real, star-struck fan. He was like, 'Oh God, I'm driving Crystal Gayle to Dublin!' He actually arrived at the hotel about two hours early so he wouldn't be late."

Getting back to the Australian tour, Byworth continues: "The last time I saw Charlie, in fact, I was touring with Crystal again. I met Charlie in Dublin and I was still really trying to push this whole Australian thing. And Charlie said, 'Look, I'm not interested, but if you want to go ahead with Dominic you've got my blessing. But you'll have to sort it out yourselves.'

"Then, tragically, he fell ill and during the first concert we did in Dunedin when Dominic was on stage, Peter McGlone, who travels with Dominic, got the phone call that Charlie had died. Obviously we couldn't tell Dominic until he'd finished the show. Charlie meant a great deal to Dominic who was really cut up.

"I can't remember whether Dominic was told before he did autographs or afterwards. But he was very upset. It wasn't entirely unexpected, because Charlie had been ill and I think the writing was on the wall. But it's not the best way to start a tour, is it?"

Recalling the onset of McBrien's illness, Dominic recalls, "It was October 1998. We were playing in Jersey, which was Charlie's last trip with me. He came to England and we had arranged the flights out to Jersey. Peter and I spent a lot of time together and we hadn't realised it at the time, but, looking back, I suppose we had noticed that Charlie was doing certain things that were just not right; things that were odd in many ways.

"Charlie flew with me to Jersey and he was complaining about flu symptoms. He wasn't feeling well and he was filling himself with tablets.

"Charlie was always the life and soul of the party. If there was ever a group of people, or a group of fans, Charlie would be in the middle stirring it up, just having a bit of fun. He was good at that and people liked him for it. "

Dominic gazes into his memories for a moment before continuing. "We got off the flight and I was waiting for my wife to come in on a flight from Belfast. One thing about Charlie was he would never leave you. He would always stay with you and he'd have a cup of tea with you at the airport. But on this occasion he just said to me, 'Look, I'm not feeling the best. Do you mind if I take a taxi to the hotel?' I said, 'Not a problem. Go ahead.' So he went on to the hotel and even though Peter and the guys were already there he didn't even acknowledge them, he just went straight on to bed. He met them later that evening and, in fact, he was late in coming down for dinner – and Charlie was never late for food.

"My wife flew over and I really didn't see a lot of Charlie that weekend. I thought he was just relaxing. He was a big Liverpool supporter and he was watching football on television. As I said, that was Charlie's last trip."

Looking back from a dressing room two years later, Dominic reaches behind him on the shelf and pulls a couple of tissues from a box to put to the corners of his eyes.

"I suppose it was a week later and he said he wasn't feeling any better. I said, 'Look, Charlie, go and see a doctor, go private, just get a check up.' To cut a long story short, Charlie was diagnosed with cancer.

"The next couple of months were hard on him. We knew things weren't good. We weren't given the whole story by his family. His family cut Peter and myself out, big time, which we were always very, very angry about. It was only afterwards that we found out the truth about his sickness; that it was worse than what we were told.

"A week before we went to Australia, I went to see him. I suppose, looking back, that I knew in my mind that it was the last time I was going to see him, and I have a great memory of that picture. It wasn't a good picture, because he was in a lot of pain. He was at home, but they were preparing him to go to hospital. They were waiting for an ambulance that day I went to see him. He was in bad, bad shape. I'll never forget that. But he opened his eyes and he spoke to me briefly, really briefly. I can still remember his last look."

Dominic pauses and takes a deep breath.

"So, we headed off. We did five shows in England, then we headed out to Australia. It was a long, long flight. We flew to Sydney, then on to Christchurch and then down to Dunedin. We had a night off in Dunedin and then we performed the next night, which happened to be the 9th of February. Remember, we were 13 hours ahead. I'd just finished my show and Peter came into the dressing room. He closed the door behind him and I thought, 'There's something not right here.'"

In a whisper, Dominic concludes, "He told me that Charlie had passed away."

Of Dominic's professionalism in the face of the tragedy, Byworth recalls, "The show had to go on. The tour had to go on, and I think having friends around him, because the band had known him a good few years and I considered myself a friend, I think that helped as well."

Looking back over the near twenty years he had known McBrien, Dominic says, "We had many ups and downs but he was very sadly missed. He was a character within the industry and a very wise man. I suppose he looked on me as a son. He was really interested and he wanted to see me doing well. He didn't want people to walk on you or anything. I probably didn't see it so much like that at the time. It's only now when I look back that I realise that. So he is very, very sadly missed."

Reflecting on McBrien's lack of involvement in the Australian tour, even before he became ill, Dominic betrays no bitterness as he explains, "When I look back at Charlie's life, he managed me within reason, but he was never a real full manager, as in a man who would have jumped in a plane, headed out to Australia and sorted the whole thing out. He wasn't that type of guy. I suppose he was more of an agent than a manager.

"So it was more my sponsors, Jim McLarnon and his wife Kath, who were interested in getting me out there. They put up the money for the flights and I did the organisation. Between three or four people we put the whole thing together. Charlie wasn't involved but he wanted me to go. He was very happy for me to go. I never had any difficulty with Charlie McBrien like that, ever. He just didn't know that market. It was out of his league, really."

Following a second New Zealand date at the Civic Theatre, Invercargill, Dominic and his entourage flew to Melbourne which became their base for four days with jaunts out to concerts in the neighbouring Geelong and Warragul, as well as Melbourne's National Theatre. Then it was on a plane to Tasmania for a show in Hobart, where the ecstatic crowd showed that Dominic's previous appearance at the Mary of Dungloe Ball had clearly not been forgotten, and two nights in Launceston in the North of the island.

The Tasmanian gigs were in luxury country club casinos and having two nights in one place should have allowed Dominic the opportunity to spend a relaxing afternoon among the acres of slot machines and roulette wheels. Instead, the hard working frequent flyer hopped on a plane back to Melbourne for a TV appearance on *Good Morning Australia,* before flying back for his evening concert.

Ten days into the tour the band enjoyed a welcome few days in Sydney where Laurie Dunn had rented some apartments in Lane Cove, a residential area on a hillside near the bay. There, they were briefly allowed the indulgences of normal tourists: basking in the heat beside a sparkling swimming pool, sightseeing and, of course, partaking of the local cuisine, and bars.

"Dominic, Peter McGlone and me all went to this Irish restaurant called Mulligans, and we all got very drunk!" recalls Byworth. "Obviously Daniel had been there before, because all around this building were O'Donnell photographs. So we insisted that Dominic's photo should take the place of Daniel's!

"I've still got the Mulligans sweatshirt they gave me a present for being such a good drinker," adds Tony, who clearly harbours fond memories of the evening. "It was probably the only night on the tour that we all went out for a little party and a meal together."

Responding to Byworth's suggestion that he got drunk at Mulligans, Dominic smiles and quietly contradicts, "No I didn't. I think we tried to get Tony drunk but he didn't fall for it -and my driver got drunk."

Although he had been handling Dominic's relationship with the press for the best part of ten years, the two trips to Australia were the first opportunity Byworth had to spend any length of time with Dominic.

Comparing the experiences of travelling with Dominic and Daniel O'Donnell, Tony reflects: "Daniel is very hard to get into. Daniel, if he's not working, will probably go back to his room. He's a solitary person. He doesn't drink. He likes his own company and if you spend a lot of time with him it can be hard going. I don't mean that nastily, but he's not really a sociable person. Whereas Dominic is like, 'Hey, we're not doing anything, we'll go out and have a few drinks somewhere.'

"He's not a heavy drinker. If he's off duty he'll have a few drinks. If he's working he won't. He might have some after the show. But the main difference is he's much more of an extrovert character. He'll spend time with you and you'll get to know him easier."

Unlike the happy to be single O'Donnell, Dominic also impressed Byworth with the strength of his devotion to his marriage, even when far from home.

"All his people are the same. All the time I was in Australia with Dominic, they were ringing up their families every night on mobile phones. Dominic would ring home after every show. Peter would ring home after every show. On mobile phones they'd taken with them from Ireland. God knows what their phone bills were."

After the stop in Sydney, it was back on the road, first to Newcastle and then a ten- hour drive north to Coolangatta where Dominic brought the tour to a triumphant close with two near sell-out nights at the Twin Towns Service Club – a towering entertainment complex with six floors of concert stages, dance floors, bars, restaurants and slot machine arcades.

It was a gruelling journey north, but worth it, not least for a welcome reunion with Louise, who had flown out with Jim and Kath McLarnon for the occasion.

During the final show, Dominic doubtless caused some pangs of jealousy among his female admirers by picking Louise out from the crowd and inviting her on stage where he serenaded her with the song *My Beautiful Wife*. Like the true gentleman he is, Dominic walked down the steps from the stage to meet her and after the song walked her back to her seat.

Looking back on Dominic's enterprising 1999 tour of Australia, Byworth concludes, "The crowds were pretty good. They weren't sell outs everywhere, but again, it was a first tour. If he had toured the year after the promo visit, or even later that same year, the crowds would have been bigger."

Sell outs or not, Dominic Kirwan again worked his magic on audiences seeing him for the first time, and received thundering standing ovations for his efforts at every venue.

Writing on the internet, Dominic's staunchest Australian fan Val Green wrote: "Dominic found out just how much we loved him Down Under when he sang *The Answer To Everything*. After the words, 'Do you love me?' the rafters shook with the reverberations of 'YES!!' We had all been watching our videos and practising."

The same fan, who claimed to have seen no fewer than five of the Australian shows, added in her review: "Later there was a medley including *Make The World Go Away, Everything Love's*

Supposed To Be and *You Are The One*, where Dominic went down into the crowd and so many lucky people had the chance to shake his hand, receive a kiss or even pinch his bum. During the shows in Melbourne and Twin Towns I wondered if he would get back on stage as the response was so great with fans calling out to him from every corner of the theatre."

Laurie Dunn, a very happy record company head, commented, "I was delighted with the response from both audiences and venue operators. Seldom does a relatively unknown performer in this market deliver such a powerful, polished show and have it greeted with standing ovations."

Wally Bishop, Dominic's Australian tour manager who had previously worked with country legends Merle Haggard, Buck Owens and Tammy Wynette, added to the chorus of approval by predicting that Dominic would "burst into superstardom in the Australian marketplace," while Sydney radio personality Tom Campbell summed up opinion with the comment that Dominic "put other visiting Irish acts in the shade."

Sadly, the tour that had begun with the death of Dominic's much loved manager Charlie McBrien had a tragic postscript for Jim and Kath McLarnon, the friends whose generosity had funded the entire venture.

"We came back," says Dominic, "and it wasn't too long after that, that I remember arriving outside a hotel in Carlisle. I got a phone call – maybe one or two in the morning, and it was from Jim to say that his daughter had died in a fire. His daughter, along with her new born-baby of six weeks. A couple of days after that, they also had a niece in Northern Ireland die in a fire. Within the same weekend."

"It really was awful," says Byworth, "It was tragic."

Looking back on his first Australian tour, Dominic says, "Laurie Dunn and his wife Ulla are wonderful people and they were very good to me. We also met a great guy who tour managed me, Wally Bishop."

It's clear Dominic retains a degree of resentment that, not only did he have to organise the tour himself, but that nobody rushed to arrange a follow-up visit that could have capitalised on his achievements while they were still fresh.

Mick Clerkin, however, defends the lack of involvement by Ritz in Dominic's Australian adventures.

"We would have to get support from the company in Australia and at the time the company we were dealing with in Australia weren't doing very well. They were about to go bust, and did go bust. We lost quite a lot of money. Then we signed to ABC, which is a very big company. As yet they have not shown any major interest (in touring Dominic) and it would have to be underwritten by the Australian company.

"It wouldn't be very beneficial for us to tour an act in another territory because we'd have nothing much to gain from it," Clerkin continues. "I mean, when we license product from here to Australia, we get back a reasonable return in terms of royalties, but it doesn't justify sending someone down and supporting them. Number One you'd have to get a promoter prepared to support it and we couldn't get that. Two, and more importantly, you've got to get a record company that will support it."

Of Australia generally, Clerkin says: "It's a very difficult market. We went down with Daniel, in conjunction with a record company that eventually went bust and it's impossible to make money in Australia. The distance between the towns and cities is so great that the cost of taking the whole crew around is astronomical. It's almost impossible to make money. And the population is very small when you consider that the UK, with 55 million people, is on our doorstep.

"Even bigger artists can't afford to go back there anymore,"

Clerkin points out. "Garth Brooks went there and he would never go back because he lost a fortune."

Of his decision, probably unique in the music business, to undertake such a foreign tour alone with neither management nor record company support, Dominic says, "Charlie McBrien didn't have the clout to move that much ahead. I was a younger man and I had that bite and the eagerness to do certain things. I was inquisitive about Australia. I still have that eagerness within the business, and I think unless you have that belief in yourself to do certain things there are many things that won't be done for you.

"Although you can prove that things can be done, it's also getting people to believe in you afterwards. And a lot of what we've done seems to have fallen on deaf ears. I suppose I've always waited for the record company to believe in me and take me back, but it's never happened."

Jim McLarnon talks enthusiastically of financing a second trip. He goes into details about advance visits to sort out the best venues. Dominic, however, is reluctant to impose a second time on the generosity of a friend.

"I know Jim would do it again," Dominic says with affection. "but I don't want to go that way. I'd prefer it if it was raised by the record company and done as part of a push behind my career."

Turning, unprompted, to investment in his career generally, Dominic continues with some passion, "I just know that if I was ever given the chance and the backing that some of the acts have been given over the years, acts that money has been squandered on. . . I feel that if money had been put into this operation, and time had been given to it a little earlier, it probably could have been on another level by now. It's doing well. But it's doing well off its own bat. The record company have been great in so far as they've been good to me and I've stayed with them. But I've had to work hard at selling the product as well."

As for returning to Australia, Dominic is keen to do so. Although plans for an autumn 2001 tour were being mooted the singer has seen too many broken promises and unfulfilled plans to hold his breath.

"There's talk about doing it again, but talk is very cheap." ■

CHAPTER TWELVE

Nashville Skyline

WITH the loss of Charlie McBrien, the priority on Dominic's return to the UK was to find a new manager.

"The Australian tour was successful for me and I enjoyed it. But I came back wondering, well, where do we go from here? I came to a cross-roads."

Given the Ritz tradition of keeping things in house, it's hardly surprising that the company's long-standing tour booker, Eamon Leahy, stepped into the breach to offer his services as Dominic's manager.

"Mick and myself, Ritz if you like, and Charlie, were always Dominic's management anyway," says Leahy. "From Day One, Dominic was one of the in-house artists that we would keep within Ritz. We looked after his concerts, the recordings, all the important stuff. Charlie looked after the dates in Ireland. But when it came to picking songs, recording and doing videos and stuff like that, it was Ritz."

There was, however, another interesting name in the frame: Cheryl Barrymore, the wife and agent behind the success of TV personality Michael Barrymore.

There can be little doubt that a well-connected, high-powered operator like Barrymore could have taken Dominic's career to another level, particularly given her contacts in the television world and Dominic's inherent appeal to the mature, family audience with which Michael Barrymore had found his prime time TV success. It could have been the perfect partnership. However, it is also easy to imagine how Barrymore could have rocked the boat of a closed institution like Ritz – and easy to see why her presence would not have been welcomed within the company.

Acknowledging the positive effect she could have had on his career, Dominic suggests Cheryl's preoccupation with the much-publicised break-up of her marriage to Michael was the reason nothing came of her brief interest in the singer. Perhaps it was simply a question of bad timing.

Tony Byworth, however, hints there could have been moves behind the scenes to prevent Dominic finding a manager who could take him away from Ritz. At the time, Byworth was still sidelined by the changed administration at Ritz, so his influence was limited. He recalls, "I felt Dominic should have a manager who was away from the Irish scene. Someone in the general entertainment field. Because I believed Dominic was a dynamic entertainer. Cheryl went to see Dominic a couple of times and I said, 'If she's interested let me go and see her. If we can swing it that's good.' But why it never followed through I don't really know. Maybe the Irish only deal with the Irish.

"I remember talking to Mick one time, which was nothing to do with Dominic," Byworth continues. "We were talking about some manager and he said, 'Aw, he's not the type of person we'd like to deal with.' Of course, he was a real go up and get 'em type manager. So I thought maybe that's what happened in relation to Dominic. I don't know. But I think Dominic was very cautious because he didn't want to fall out with the record label."

Elaborating on the cronyism that dominated the political

agenda at Ritz, Byworth points out that, "Charlie McBrien and a lot of these guys were all mates of Mick Clerkin. Sean Riley who manages Daniel was a mate of Mick's. There was a singer on the label called John Hogan, and his manager was a friend of Mick's. They all knew each other.

"Eamon actually fell out with Mick briefly, although they're friends again now, over the plc business. So he left Ritz and took over Dominic's management."

Byworth's suggestion that "maybe the Irish only deal with the Irish," is lent some weight by Scotsman Jim Rosie who worked for many years as compère and road manager with Daniel O'Donnell and other Ritz acts including Dominic.

"The Irish are a group of people who can climb a ten-rung ladder and when they get to the tenth rung they go over it," says Rosie. "Everybody else, no matter who you are, will only get to the ninth rung. You will never know how they work and how they react and how they do things. They'll tell you, and you'll see things, but deep down the Irish are a totally independent group of people. I could never say at the end of the day I know them truly."

Eamon Leahy got into the music business by sheer bravado. Coming from a background of hotel management, the Irishman was working as deputy manager of the Albany hotel in Glasgow, the main stop over for music executives on business in Scotland. In particular, Leahy became friendly with Jeff Gilbert of CBS who one day told him he was looking to recruit a man to represent the company in Scotland and the North East of England. To the record man's surprise, Leahy said, 'I could do that.' And, to Leahy's surprise, Gilbert took him up on it, inviting him to an interview in London.

True to his claim, Eamon proved a great success in his new position and became the company's rep for Scotland. When CBS closed its Scottish office, Leahy moved to RCA. By that time he was also covering Northern Ireland, which is where he first met Mick Clerkin at the time when Ritz was enjoying Irish success with the Gloria single, *One Day At A Time* but finding it impossible to secure a UK release for the song. When Clerkin's original partner in Ritz, Peter Dempsey, died soon after the formation of the company, Clerkin invited Eamon to join Ritz as a director to handle the tour bookings of his artists.

It was an unusual arrangement. As Byworth observes, "Ritz was probably the only record company booking tours."

In the music business generally, record companies, managers and tour promoters tend to be distinct and separate entities with each fighting their own corner. At Ritz, everything was in house. Everything was under control.

Leahy says, "When Dominic came back from Australia, he was a little bit in limbo because of all the changes at Ritz at the time. The company had become a plc and had acquired the Grapevine label which had its own agenda with singers like Sinead Logan and Mary Black and Dominic was put slightly on the back burner. Daniel had Mick fighting his corner through his involvement in Daniel's management company, Brockwell, and I thought Dominic should have somebody fighting his corner at Ritz.

"I didn't know about Cheryl Barrymore," Leahy continues, "but I knew there were a lot of Irish band promoters chasing after him and that wouldn't have helped his situation as far as Ritz was concerned."

Surprisingly, Dominic says, "Eamon is not really a manager as such. He's more of a booking agent. The management is something I see which needs to be a complete team effort these days, rather than being one single person.

"But Eamon approached me and said 'We've been working together for years, I've been doing things for you on going, would you be interested. . .' So we talked about management. We talked about sitting down and at least working out some structure."

Eamon's first move on taking the reins was to propose that,

after a decade of recording domestically, the artist should make his first album in the country music capital of Nashville, Tennessee. His decision was prompted by the song *Unconditional Love* which became the title track of Dominic's first American produced record. A little-known Glen Campbell album track, *Unconditional Love* had been suggested to Dominic a year previously by Al Moir, a teacher and part-time *Country Music People* journalist.

"Al sent me a collection of songs he thought might interest me. I listened to different tracks and it just leapt out at me," says Dominic, "I always remember thinking, it's a song I want to do.

"I'd also heard the song *Don't Break The Heart That Loves You* from Ritz. When we started talking about recording the next album and what vein we would go in I played these tracks to Eamon and he suggested, 'I think Nashville would be good for this.'

"I suppose I took it with a pinch of salt, and then about three weeks later, Eamon phoned me and said, 'It looks as if it's going to happen.' That was probably the latter end of March. Within a couple of weeks we were sitting around a table with Gerry Crowley of Ritz. We were talking about songs, preparing the album and, lo and behold, I was on my way to Nashville."

The Mr Fix-it for the venture was Tony Byworth, who was brought back into the picture by Clerkin.

"Mick would have been embarrassed by it," says Byworth, of his falling out with Ritz before Dominic's Australian tour. "But the company wasn't in his hands anymore. There was a board of directors and a CEO and he wanted to run things his way. So I just backed away from the whole thing. Me and Dominic got on with our Australian tour. But Mick was concerned. He wanted me to be involved and, as Dominic was a friend, when we came back from Australia Mick rang me up and said would I look after the Nashville recordings. He said, 'That might help to get you doing some work with Ritz again.'"

A decade previous, in the same year that Dominic joined Ritz, Byworth had been responsible for brokering the deal that saw O'Donnell record his first Nashville album under producer Alan Reynolds. At the time, Reynolds was known for his work with Crystal Gayle and Don Williams. But he was about to go on to enjoy his greatest success with American superstar-to-be Garth Brooks.

Byworth had since co-ordinated Nashville recording projects for Ritz artists Sarah Jory, John Hogan and Charley Pride, who had signed to Ritz after losing his label affiliation in the States. Dominic says: "I never saw Nashville as being any part of my project. I suppose like many people I'd been cynical about it. I'm not into this cowboy hat, guns and holsters syndrome and I probably had that perception of it. I had also heard recordings that had been made on that side of the world for other Irish acts and I thought they were not getting what the Americans could get. So I was apprehensive about it all. I thought, 'What's the point in going out that far and not getting what you're looking for?'

"In the back of my mind I thought it would be nice to go along and just take a look around. But on both occasions I wouldn't have had much time to do any discovering. It's all been working."

The Nashville sessions were booked for the 9-17 of June, 1999, when the city would be buzzing with the annual feast of concerts and autograph signing sessions that is Fan Fair. The producer was Ronny Light, who had worked on the Pride, Hogan and Jory albums.

The arrangements followed the blueprint laid down by Jory's 1995 visit, with Dominic booked into the Hampton Inn and the recordings split between The Reflections Studio, in the Berry Hills district, where the band tracks would be recorded, and Ronny's more intimate home studio, which he calls The Lighthouse, and where he prefers to capture vocals and mix the final tracks.

"It's an amazing place," says Byworth of The Lighthouse. "It looks rough and ready, but all the equipment there is wonderful stuff. Ronny will actually go into another studio and take equipment from his house that is better than the studio equipment."

In a memo to Clerkin dated May 10, Byworth detailed Dominic's itinerary:

Tuesday, June 8 -Arrive in Nashville. June 9 -Meeting with Ronny Light. June 10 & 11 -Cutting tracks at Reflections Studio. June 12 & 13 Days off. June 14-17 -Recording vocals.

In the event, however, The Reflections studio was dropped in favour of Hilltop Studios, on the outskirts of Goodlettsville to the north of the city. A tape of the songs Dominic was due to record was mailed to Ronny along with a selection of Dominic's previous recordings with which the producer was to familiarise himself.

"Ronny doesn't like to go in cold," says Byworth, "so he wanted a couple of days ahead of the session so he could go out with Dominic. I'd introduce them and then I would disappear so he could spend the day with Dominic and get to know him.

"When I take an artist to Nashville, the first day is off while you acclimatise yourself and get over the jet lag. The second day you spend with Ronny and then the third day you go into the studio."

Famed for a ghostly grey pallor gained by working long hours in dark studios, Light began his career playing guitar for country legend Eddy Arnold, who between 1945 and 1983 enjoyed the most successful run on the country charts of any singer in history. Light's first visit to England saw him appearing at one of the famed Wembley Festivals where he was part of the Skeeter Davis band. Throughout the Seventies Light was a staff producer for RCA in Nashville, where he produced records by artists including Waylon Jennings, Bobby Bare, Skeeter Davis and others before turning freelance.

Among Light's first independent productions were albums by troubled and fading American country singer Tommy Collins and the little known pairing of Gary Lumpkin & Connie Lee Stich, whom he recorded for a short-lived label set up by Englishman Craig Baguley.

Coincidentally, Baguley succeeded Byworth as editor of Britain's long established country music magazine, *Country Music People*, which Byworth had edited from 1977 to 1983. It was Baguley who suggested to Byworth that Light would be the perfect producer for the first album that Charley Pride recorded for Ritz, especially as Pride was one of the few RCA artists Light had not worked with during his stint on the label. The result was the Ritz album *Classics With Pride* and an enduring and productive friendship between Byworth and Light. Never the cheapest or least picky of producers, Allan Reynolds had ceased to be an option for Ritz, following his world beating success with Garth Brooks.

Dominic's first impression of Ronny was that he was very quiet and interested in people. "He was very professional in his approach to music and what he wanted to do, and more than helpful in every aspect.

"I suppose sincerity was what I spotted in him immediately so I knew from that moment on that I was gonna have a rapport with this guy."

"In the studio he's great to work with. He's done his homework. He's prepared. He's obviously sussed me well enough. He has a fair idea of what he wants to hear and what the final product's going to be. I suppose that's his professionalism from years of working at RCA. That came through within a day or two."

Light assembled a crack team of seasoned studio musicians for the sessions. Dominic says, "I was introduced to Milton Sledge and I knew immediately I'd heard his name before. He works in the studio with Garth Brooks. I was introduced to David Smith who has worked with Gene Watson and a lot of other acts. Leo Jackson, who was one of Jim Reeves' original Blue Boys. So I knew the names and it was like being a punter. You walk in and think, 'These guys have worked with the big names. They are something special.' Yet, when you say hello and sit down and feel more relaxed with them, you find they're all human beings. They're all there for a purpose and that's to make music and do it to the best of their ability. So, like my meeting with Ronny I started to feel secure with the guys in the band. Once that happened it was plain sailing."

The recording process was a new one to Dominic. Nashville is one of the last musical cities on Earth where complete bands of musicians play live together in the studio.

"In Birmingham, Terry Bradford would start with a basic rhythm track, basically just drums and bass, then work on a vocal and a performance. Then the track would be built around it. In Nashville you work for the first couple of days laying the rhythm tracks with the whole band; drums, bass, lead guitar, acoustic guitar and keyboards. So I actually got the feel of a live performance. That's your basics. And it's like building a house. As long as you've got the foundations right you've got something to work with.

"Once the tracks were down, the band was finished and I didn't see them again. Then it was into the studio, just me and the producer, to do the vocals."

One advantage of Light's method was that Dominic came away from each day's recording with a tape of his finished vocal accompanied by a fairly full backing. Even though Light would make many finishing touches to the album after Dominic left Nashville, including recording harmony vocals and additional instrumental parts, and mixing the final sound, Dominic says, "I'd have a fair idea of what the track was going to sound like, and maybe even surmise what Ronny was going to do with certain things. Whereas the other way around I didn't, because I'd just left it as drums and bass."

Dominic insists that "Vocals are all about the voice being rested, being prepared and having a fair idea of what you're looking for. After that it's down to the producer listening and catching what the performance is about.

"Most singers would only do a vocal a day, and that was the way I worked in Birmingham, but because I was only in Nashville for a couple of weeks, I ended up having to do two, maybe three a day, providing I was feeling relaxed enough to get a good performance. You could probably perform the song 10 or 15 times before you get a good vocal. Or, in some cases, you might get a really good vocal the first time but Ronny would make you sing it a few times and from that you might catch a better line. So you would what they call fly in certain lines. That goes on in the music industry all the time."

For the final word on when a vocal was finished, Dominic always deferred to Light.

"To hear the dry vocal as they call it can be kinda scary. I'm sure I'm like many other acts in that I don't listen to my voice. I'm not saying I don't like it, but when you hear your own voice you tend to think, 'Is that what I sound like?' Other people hear you in a different way. I listen to my producer and I listen for advice. I know on the far side of the studio he's hearing what he's looking for or he's not hearing it and he's going to tell me whether it's right or wrong. I put a lot of faith in these people. I would also tell them that if there's anything dubious we have to do it again. That's how we build that rapport."

One observer of Dominic's studio technique, Tony Byworth says, "He's got a good ear. He can pick up on a song very quickly, and you know fairly soon whether it's going to work or not. With some people you play around for hours and then decide it's not going to work. With Dominic you can sense whether it's going to happen or not.

"Ronny got on very well with him in the studio. They laid down all the rough tracks on 18 songs in two days. Nashville musicians work very well and we're not talking about the most complicated songs you ever heard in your life, but they did that very quickly.

"Occasionally with Dominic his voice goes," Byworth adds. "On that first time in Nashville we had a day when he just couldn't sing. It's frightening when you've got a deadline and you're trying to finish an album.

"In Australia, knowing that his voice gets stressed, we made sure that every so often there was a day off. It was more expensive that way, but he needed it. That way he could control his voice. I don't think he misses concerts because of it. He knows if he's got to work he'll probably do less talking. But he does have a weakness."

Despite the trouble he'd had with his voice during the recording of *The Music's Back*, Dominic shrugs off the day he couldn't sing during the *Unconditional Love* sessions.

"I got tired. The travelling and the jet lag and everything. It was all new to me. I went into it very smart about it, thinking this is the way to do it. I felt relaxed so I just went for it. But there was a day when I just woke up and I knew that day would not be a good day for me vocally. As a singer you know these things. So I had to take a rest. It wasn't a panic. If I'd had to stay another day or two it would have had to be done."

As ever, *Unconditional Love*, included several covers. Among the familiar material was the opening *I Tell It Like It Used To Be*, a big, hooky, honky tonk flavoured ballad and former hit for the once promising New Country singer T. Graham Brown. Other covers included George Strait's recent hit *We Really Shouldn't Be Doing This*, and the standards *Through The Years, Your Love Amazes Me* and *Sometimes When We Touch*. In each case, however, Dominic made the material fully his own, prompting Craig Baguley, reviewing the disc in *Country Music People*, to write ". . .a cover of

We Really Shouldn't Be Doing This I enjoyed more than the great Strait's version."

Dominic is a George Strait fan. Of that particular song he says, "I knew immediately it would be good for stage. It's a tempting, teasing song for stage, you know? There's a bit of the devil in me as the man says and once I heard the words of the song I thought it would be good for the show. So that song was really selected for show purposes and not for becoming a hit record or anything like that."

Byworth reckons Dominic is good at picking material. "He's got a good sense of what suits him and what doesn't. He's always interested in listening to new songs. You'll take him a song and he'll say, 'Yeah, I'll have a listen to it.' Because I think he's looking at his career in the long term. He wants to move on. He wants to be successful. So he's going to listen to stuff.

"I think if the truth be known, he may have been getting a little weary of cover jobs for Ritz. My one criticism of Dominic's albums, and he knows I know it, is I would spend more time finding original songs. The way of working at Ritz is they tend to do covers. But I don't think you're ever going to be a major star if you exist on covers.

"Dominic carries his career a lot. He has certain ideas and, as far as the records are concerned, he will have input into it. But he also listens to the record company because they've got to market it.

"As far as the first Nashville album was concerned, they already had most of the material selected. Ronny Light had come up with one or two suggestions. But most of it was laid down. Then you'd go in the studio and see if it worked and if it didn't work you'd kick it out, rather quickly, and move on to another song.

"Using bluegrass singer Rhonda Vincent on the duet *The Right Time Of The Night*, came about because Ronny is a long-time friend of hers and a dedicated advocate of her music. He's probably her prime promoter. Initially we picked *Sometimes When We Touch*, which Tammy Wynette had recorded as a duet with Mark Gray. But it just didn't work. Their voices didn't blend.

"But I thought having Rhonda involved was a good little plus in selling the record. So we used her on *Right Time Of The Night* instead, and that worked. In fact, they never met each other. Rhonda was out on the road. So we recorded bits of it and Ronny mixed Rhonda's bit in after Dominic had gone back to the UK. I'm just sorry Ritz didn't make more of it, because it was a good song. But then I wasn't speaking to Ritz, so I had nothing to do with the marketing."

Dominic wasn't fazed about singing a duet with a singer he'd never met, observing, "The strangest part would be if you met her tomorrow and you know you've worked with her but you've never met her. That would be strange. But that's the way the industry is. You have to take a lot of this in your stride because the technology has taken over many things. You have to leave your mind open to that."

As for the choice of Vincent, Dominic shrugs. "We had talked about various acts. Ronny said, 'I know this girl personally and I can get her to do it. What do you think?' I said, 'Not a problem.' It didn't really matter to me. But it was nice to have someone from Nashville, or America should I say, on the album. It just gave it a different punch."

Another singer whom Dominic didn't meet was Claire Lynch, who added harmony vocals to her composition *Friends For A Lifetime*.

"Trionogh Moore, who was my backing vocalist at the time, had suggested that I should listen to Claire, and I just liked the song. Admittedly, Claire had written it for her son, so it was really a mother talking to her son, but I liked the sentiments of the song so we changed the lyrics around to suit a man." Responding to the suggestion that *Friends For A Lifetime* suits him because it sounds more like an Irish song than an American composition, Dominic adds, "Claire comes from a bluegrass background and if you listen to bluegrass you'll find a lot of Irish influences."

Fan Fair is Nashville's most popular week of the year in terms of tourism with tens of thousands flocking from all over America and across the Atlantic to attend country music's most concentrated gathering of stars. Sadly, Dominic was unable to join the throng.

"I wanted to get to Fan Fair. I had a backstage pass, but the studio was so important I couldn't spare the time."

In his few brief moments of downtime, Dominic was able to hook up and compare notes with Charlie Landsborough, who was also in Nashville to record. Towards the end of his visit Dominic also spared an evening to accompany Ronny to one of Nashville's most famous venues and songwriter haunts, The Bluebird Cafe.

Writer Steve Seskin was performing an acoustic set and Dominic found one of the songs that was to become one of the highlights of his next Nashville album. The song was *Don't Laugh At Me:* a dignified plea for respect in the voice of various down trodden members of society, ranging from children picked on for wearing glasses or braces on their teeth, to a homeless man reduced to begging in the streets after a drunken driver killed his wife.

"He performed it just himself and a guitar and I related to the song immediately." says Dominic. "I thought, 'I know every word in this song.' It reminded me of *The Streets of London.* That's really what it was all about. As I was sitting there I remembered an occasion when my wife and I had been in London. We'd come out of a theatre and we were walking down the street and there was a soup van out late at night. They were handing out teas and coffees and whatever, and I remember seeing this old guy laying in a corner with a beret on. I thought, well, here's a guy who probably fought for his country and he is on the streets with no home. And the bullying that goes on in life through schools. . ." Dominic gazes for a moment into his own troubled schooldays. "I thought lots of parts of life were in that song and I could relate to it. Straight away I wanted to record it."

Dominic thought the Bluebird was something special. "I love the whole thing of a venue where you can go and hear songs from scratch. You hear it from the writer themselves and how they feel. There have been many hit songs over the years that have been written and the original has never been heard. When I say the original, I'm talking about the composer. When you hear it from somebody like that in a place like The Bluebird where they have contact with the audience, talk about songs and how they felt about it and why they wrote it, you can probably understand it a lot better, and that's relevant to everything that you do afterwards. The Bluebird captured everything I felt the music industry is about and we should know more about."

Critically, *Unconditional Love* was without doubt Dominic's best received album to date.

Even sceptics were won over. Giving *Unconditional Love* a four out of five star rating in *Country Music People*, editor Craig Baguley began an enthusiastic review with the words, "I have never been a fan of Dominic Kirwan's voice until now. . . Ronny Light has brought out the man's strengths and allied them to some cracking material." Concluding five paragraphs of unreserved praise, Baguley finished: "Dominic Kirwan is more Tom Jones than Texas but *Unconditional Love* comes as a nice surprise. It's his best album by far, and suggests he should view Nashville as a permanent recording base. Congratulations to all involved."

The album also picked up the Best Album Home & Abroad trophy in the UK Radio Awards.

Dominic's man in radio land, Mike Perry, reports: "*Unconditional Love* was very well received. He got lots of airplay on that one. *Let Me Romance You* and *Step Aside Or Love Me Tonight* were very big songs from that album. Radio did love that one. Because it was up tempo, and it's got a lot of brass on it. Generally, I speak to his fans and they do like his up tempo stuff, because he wiggles the old hips and dances around . I mean, they like the ballads, but they like to see him move."

Looking back on the album, Dominic says, "It's one of the best I've done. I suppose I have a certain thing in my mind about how an album should sound. That's your own personal thing and you've got to get that across to your producers. When you do a show and someone comes up and says, 'That was a great performance but it doesn't sound the same on the record,' that's the thing you're always looking for. Because records are different from live performances. They're a lot more refined. So it's difficult to get that. But I felt that what I was doing vocally were close enough to what I wanted to hear. That was important to me.

"I realised this guy is picking out of this voice of mine exactly what I hear myself. That has to be something special. That's what Nashville has done for me." ■

CHAPTER THIRTEEN

Live From Galway

FRIDAY. It must be Broxbourne – a soulless cluster of boxy housing developments and pedestrianised zones just outside of the M25. A no-man's land lost between the suburbs and the provinces. Dampened by sparse but irritating spots of rain, the Civic Hall is a modern red brick building set low in a curious hollow behind the older town hall and some miserable looking flats. The only sign of the venue from the road is a battered notice board. There are posters for children's entertainer Charlie & The Jelly Factory and Calamity Jane by the East Herts Operatic Society. Between them is the smiling face of Dominic Kirwan, a water stain on the poster slightly disfiguring his handsome features.

Inside the foyer a receptionist is reading the local paper behind the desk. Beside the entrance to the bar, Dominic's merchandise stand is still packed up in the battered black flight case that once belonged to another Irish singer, Christy Moore. In the basement dressing room, Ali is unpacking and hanging up Dominic's stage wear.

Above her head, the 500 seats of the auditorium will not be filled with the faithful for another four hours, but the band, casually dressed, are on stage, finishing off their sound check.

One of the overhead lights is wrongly angled, so a technician comes on stage with a hi-tech piece of equipment to fix it – an enormous pole with which he taps the offending light into position. As the man with the pole emerges from the wings, Jim McVeigh begins playing the Laurel & Hardy theme tune. The rest of the band spontaneously join in, a crackle of barely restrained creative energy running between them.

"We're just going to try something," Jim says into his microphone once the light has been adjusted.

In the aisle at the side of the auditorium, Dominic is wearing a light green suit. His part of the sound check complete, he's chatting to a couple of guests about the house he's having built on the outskirts of Omagh. Explaining that he's not moving that far into the countryside he points across the rows of seats and says, "The next house would be no further away than that wall."

As he speaks, a strange yet strangely familiar piece of music suddenly erupts from the stage. Dominic cracks up. "Listen to that!" He shouts above the music. The reggae version of *Unconditional Love!*

In the dressing room shortly after, Dominic is asked if he will be doing the reggae version on stage later that night.

He says "No, but it's something for us to have fun with."

When his guests have gone, however, Dominic begins to wonder, Why not? All through his show that evening, he keeps looking at the band, keeping them guessing about the dare on his mind. Finally, he lets them unveil their creative masterpiece in public for the first time. The response from the audience is so great that the reggae version becomes a regular part of the show. So much so that a few weeks later in Inverness Dominic receives a large, mysterious parcel. One of his fans has gone to a theatrical shop and bought him a large Rastafarian style hat complete with trailing dreadlocks. From that point, there's no going back.

A month later, Dominic is drinking tea in the cafeteria of

another theatre and discussing the amazing popularity of *Unconventional Unconditional* as the number has become known. Peter McGlone thinks that it should be released as a single.

"You better not do it in Brixton," says their guest.

Of course, there is nothing racially offensive about Dominic's performance. "But, hastily swallowing his tea," he admits, "I was in Birmingham the other week. I started doing the song and I suddenly thought – Uh-oh, I'm in Birmingham! But they loved it. "

Gloria Hunniford crossed one black nylon-clad knee over the other and leaned towards the camera of her Channel Five afternoon show, *Open House.* With the distinctive Irish accent that had once, coincidentally, made a little-known album for Ritz, she told the viewers, "Our next guest is a hugely popular singer whose albums have twice taken the top spot in the British country music charts. Over the years he has built up such a dedicated audience that they've even launched a petition demanding that he appear more often on British television. "

Sitting back to tighten her pink jacket around her waist, Gloria added with a smile, "Well, 40,000 fans can't be wrong, so will you please give a warm welcome to Dominic Kirwan! "

"I couldn't believe 40,000 people would put their name to a petition," said Dominic when, dressed in black and looking as sharp as a razor he flopped on to the couch beside his hostess. "But I'm very grateful that they did."

Forty thousand. Fan Moira Clydesdale had been busy since she first gathered 700 signatures to get Dominic on *Style Challenge,* circulating petition forms among fans across the length and breadth of the country.

"They started writing to TV shows and it snowballed," says Promotions man Mike Perry who liaised with Moira on which shows she petitioned. "We got one or two televisions on the back of that. Gloria mentioned it. A couple of years before that, *After Five* mentioned it."

"It worked within reason," reflects Dominic. "I suppose it hasn't been 100percent. We did get a couple of national things but nothing major."

"We don't play on it so much now," says Perry, "because you can only do it once or twice. Sometimes it alienates people as well. It's like you are just trying to twist arms to put him on because of these signatures. But at the time it was quite genuine."

Dominic claims that there is a cynicism that runs through the TV world. "If you get on these guys nerves they'll put you aside. It's kinda frightening at times. You don't want to overstep the boundaries but, at the same time, to have people talk about you, to believe in what you do, and to go to the extremes that they've gone has to be something special."

Despite such massive demonstrations of public support, however, the difficulty getting Dominic on mainstream television remains as tough, if not tougher, than ever. Perry looks after O'Donnell, David Essex and Joe Longthorn,. "Even with Daniel it's all governed by the charts and who's hip. They all want the glitzy stars. So it's hard for people in Dominic's genre to get mainstream TV. "

Sponsor Kath McLarnon sums up the frustration of television fans across the UK . " When you sit here at night and watch the rubbish that you have to watch, why can't they have somebody like Dominic on?"

Perry claims that Dominic has done quite well over the years with five or six network shows. He's done Granada, Yorkshire, Anglia. . . and he gets lots of fan mail. He's one of the most popular artists when he goes on TV and does the regions. But nationally it's a drawback when you haven't had a big chart album or a top ten single. There are many young producers nowadays who aren't aware of Dominic's popularity.

Perry approached the *Brian Connolly Show* "But they said we've got Geri Halliwell, Ronan Keating, Emma Bunton. . . the predictable, current, flavour-of-the-month pop artists. No one seems to want to take a chance or gamble with someone like Dominic who is a great artist and has lots of appeal, because he hasn't had chart success."

Unfortunately, Dominic came a little bit late, according to Clerkin. "In the early days when we had The Fureys and Foster & Allen, they were both well played on Radio 2 and they appeared on *Top Of The Pops*, as did Daniel. But then Radio 2 changed their music policy and it became more difficult to get people like Dominic on there. I mean, we can't even get Daniel played on Radio 2 any more. I refer to Radio 2 now as Radio One & A Half.

"Regional radio has been very good to us, but even on regional radio they tend to pigeon hole music. Oh, that's Dominic Kirwan, that's country, which, in most cases, Dominic's not. That's for the guy who presents the country show, and he comes in twice a week or maybe once a week in some cases. With normal daytime play, with the exception of some areas like Scotland and East Anglia, exposure is hard to come by. It makes our job very difficult."

Dominic's appearance on Gloria Hunniford's *Open House*, singing *Step Aside* or *Love Me Tonight*, proved once again that when he did find himself in front of the cameras he was superb. The same point was made by appearances on BBC1s *Songs Of Praise* and Anglia's equivalent, *Sunday Morning Show*.

A selection of performances from the latter series were gathered on the Ritz video *Amazing Grace* which featured Dominic singing *Bless This House* and *You Are The One* alongside performances by O'Donnell, Landsborough, Michael English, Mary Duff and, one of the label's more unusual signings, the country 'n' operatic Finbar Wright who contributed the Pavarotti favourite *O Sole Mio*.

In addition to individual studio performances, the highlight was a live performance at Frinton Free Church by Dominic, Daniel, Charlie and Mary. Having dueted with the demurely suited Duff on *What A Friend We Have In Jesus,* the black-suited

Dominic led the quartet, and the local congregation, in the finale of *How Great Thou Art*. Landsborough would have made a stronger impression if he had learned his verse instead of reading it off the page. But it was nevertheless a fine piece of television that surely suggested all of the Ritz performers deserved a regular place in the nation's viewing schedules. Especially in an age of multiple terrestrial, satellite and cable channels when viewer choice is the supposed buzz word.

"I do have this feeling that something has to give," says Dominic. "Not only for me. I've looked at it now and thought to myself, well, you've got a fair bit out of this business. It's been good to me and hopefully it will be good to me for years to come. But there's a part of me that keeps saying, you cannot close down on people. I don't know how you get to the powers that be and make them realise that there are a lot of good acts out there, and so many people who want to watch certain things on television and listen to it on the radio. You cannot alienate all those people.

"That's what I would pick out of what these people (who signed the petition) have done and what they believe in."

In the meantime, with TV fame as elusive as ever, it was back to his more reliable places of work: the road and the studio.

"Once I got *Unconditional Love* out and we had the rapport with the audience and knew that it had worked, it was only a matter of time before we were starting to talk of the next album and what we were going to do with it. Once that talk started I don't think it took us long to decide that it had to be Nashville again," says Dominic.

Before he returned to Music City for his next studio album, however, Ritz decided to release a new video, *Live From Galway*. Dominic had reservations about the idea. Having already made three performance videos he would prefer to do a location one. "I'd like to sit down and be interviewed about life and why certain songs were picked or whatever. So that's something that maybe in time we'll be able to do.

"But it was five years since we had recorded a video. They were planning to do a television series of Irish country music and we were approached to be part of that. It was probably Eamon Leahy who suggested we should use the opportunity of the facilities to record a video. We knew our audience was looking for something new, so I agreed. And it was a good thing to do because we learned from the sales that the audience were definitely hungry for something new. "

If any of Dominic's fans were disappointed with the decision to release *Live From Galway* it was those who had bought tickets to be part of a video scheduled to be shot at the Stardust Club in Leicester. Some of them had made a point of being in the audience for all of Dominic's videos up to that point and were taken unawares by the speed with which the shoot was switched to Ireland.

"The original plan was to do it at the Stardust because it was more of a cabaret thing," admits Dominic, "but then the facilities were there in Galway and, bang, we were in the middle of it. It was nothing to do with the Stardust. To me, the Stardust would still be a good place to use."

A CD, also called *Live From Galway* but with a slightly different track listing, was released at the same time as the video. It was intended as a cheap, throwaway piece of merchandising. It turned out to be one of the most powerful recordings of Dominic's career.

Nobody was trying to make great art. Nobody was worrying about every note. And precisely because of those things, the full magic of Dominic's live performance was captured in a way that his recent albums had only hinted at. Dominic was in top form vocally and, more importantly, he and the band had lived and worked with the material long enough to become one with it. Songs like *Unconditional Love, Sometimes When We Touch* and *Friends For A Lifetime*, which Dominic had performed for the first time when he recorded them in Nashville the previous year were now fully worn in and rendered with an intimacy and suppleness that left the studio versions sounding stiff.

The live recordings of earlier songs such as *I Swear* and *Please Release Me* also outstripped the earlier album cuts while other songs, such as crowd pleasing covers of *If I Said You Had A Beautiful Body* and *Dance The Night Away*, were made available on a Dominic Kirwan CD for the first time.

"To Ritz it was a throwaway album," says Terry Bradford, who was brought back into Dominic's career to mix the CD.

"I often wondered why they were putting out compilations between real albums. They were watering down the main thing. But by that time I think Ritz as a company were struggling. They needed to get product out and those sorts of things turn over.

"I'd not been involved with Dominic for some time, but I was phoned up by the record company and they said they had an opportunity of doing a cheap, simple album. Would I go over and make sure it went down on tape and would I mix it for them?

Bradford recalls the final part of his brief: "How cheap could I do it for?!"

"It's completely live, mistakes and all," says Dominic, "There's a big mistake in the middle and we didn't fix it. Really, we couldn't have fixed it, because we would have had to go back and do the whole set again. I suppose the director should have stopped it, but he didn't, and it was only an hour later that I thought about it. The mistake is in *If I Said You Had A Beautiful Body*. I sing the same verse twice. Only two people have noticed that.

"I'm happy how it turned out, but I still feel I can always do better. But that's just me. After every project I think, well, now the next one has to be better again. That's how I look at life."

The highlight of *Live From Galway* is Dominic's version of *The Town I Love So Well*, a song that had become a show-stopping part of his concerts, generating spontaneous standing ovations wherever he travelled.

Although Phil Coulter's song refers to Derry it took on a special significance for Dominic after the Omagh atrocity. "Because it's about people and how they live in the everyday way of life, striving for a lasting peace, I found it to be a song which reflected how I felt.

"It is a challenge to perform such an epic piece of material. It's a difficult song because it's important and well written. When you get something as strong as that it is hard to sing. There are people out there who have performed things like this and they should never have touched it. That's not a slag in any way. I just feel that with a song like that, people have to understand what it's about.

"The first time I performed it after I left Omagh was the first day of some of the burials in my home town. I'd seen it only on the television because I'd had to leave the town and start work again. I remember singing it in Scotland and I broke down. But then, everybody broke down, because it was so much on the minds of everyone, Scottish, English, Welsh. "

The nature of *The Town I Love So Well* found Dominic breaking new ground as an artist and moving beyond the realms of easy listening. The singer, however, does not see singing the song as a major departure. Neither does he see it as courting political controversy. "*The Town I Love So Well* is a song for me and I don't see why I shouldn't sing it.

"There's a cynical attitude among a few people in Northern Ireland and, for that matter, throughout the UK. Some people will put that down as a political song, but they really are not listening to the words which are telling a story. Yes, it does talk about the army being installed by the gas yard wall. But that's only stating a fact. It's not getting at the army. It talks about the guns and the tanks and the bombs. That's all true. Everything was on the streets. So the song talks about the army being on the streets. . . the bombs by the terrorists. The song is respectful to all attitudes and all parts of society. Yet there is always a minority who will look at it and say it is a political song.

"Again, it comes back to listening to the words. It's a man speaking about his town. About how the people lived. How he got the opportunity to go away and become successful and come back and see the changes. And yet, no matter what changes were there, and no matter how much he remembered about the past, the one common denominator was the lasting peace that they were seeking and striving for."

If a single album captures the magnitude, breadth and depth of Dominic's talent it is *Live From Galway*. Sadly, for Terry Bradford, the album will always be associated with more personal memories.

"It's poignant for me because while I was there my mother died. I had a feeling when I left that I was never going to see her again. She was not very well. She said, 'Look, I'm fine, go. You don't have to feel guilty. You don't have to worry or anything.' And yet I knew when I went that it would be the last time I saw her.

"Because we were very close, she got me out of the way. I know it sounds daft. But I could not have handled being here."

Before Dominic boarded the plane that would take him back to Nashville to make his next album, the singer found himself on another plane. . . to an unknown destination for a surprise birthday present courtesy of his wife and the McLarnons.

"I'd always said I didn't want to be around for my 40th birthday. One of the reasons is because I live in a localised region. If you switch on television or you switch on the radio there's always somebody who will remind me about a birthday. So I just said to my wife a long time ago that I didn't want to be around on the day."

"We took him to Cyprus as a surprise," says Kath McLarnon.

"I didn't know where I was going," says Dominic, Louise told him he was going on two flights. First to London and then somewhere after that. "When I got to London, Jim and Kath were waiting for me. . . "

When they got to Cyprus they had a wonderful time. And, amazingly, even around the pool people knew him! There was someone from Ireland, and from Wales. The McLarnons had a further surprise up their sleeves.

"We had Peter McGlone fly from Dublin," says Jim. "He arrived at the hotel about five hours later and we made sure we kept Dominic awake until he arrived."

"It was a hassle for weeks before," recalls Kath, "Doing his passport and everything. We got Ritz to work around it so he'd have some days off. They all knew Louise was taking him somewhere, but nobody knew where. But he enjoyed it. He's always saying if he gets a break he'll go back again."

"It was a nice surprise," says Dominic. "Growing up in Omagh, my mother and father did everything for me, but we were not a family that went away on summer holidays and things like that. We went mainly on day trips. So it was only later in life that I started travelling away on holiday. . ."

Returning to Nashville for the next album could hardly be described as a holiday. But at least his second visit to Music City gave him time for a sightseeing trip to Memphis. Priority was a visit to Graceland, home of the late king of rock'n'roll.

Dominic admits: "Elvis is Elvis. To me he was the epitome of what entertainment is about. He was able to perform most styles of music, be it blues, rock'n'roll or ballads. That's what an artist is all about. So to go to where he lived for the main part of his life, to where he recorded, is something special. Something I'll never forget.

"Graceland is commercial and there are thousands visiting Graceland every day. But I never get caught up in commercialism because I respect the place and know what it's about. People like certain mementoes of where they've been but I'm very good at cutting all that out and looking at the facts. The facts for me were the home where he lived and the rooms he worked in. Particularly the Jungle Room where he would have done a lot of recording, the music rooms. And he lived a very modest life. From the roadside it looks like a mansion but it's not as big as it's made out to be. Seeing these things was important to me."

Dominic also visited the legendary Sun Records studio on Union Avenue where Elvis began his career and where in fact, almost the whole of white rock'n'roll was born.

"You drive towards Sun Studios and it looks exactly like the days when Elvis was there. They might have done some things to the inside but definitely not the outside. The original studio's still there. All the wooden floor, the wooden panelling. It's the studio they would have stood in: Carl Perkins, Johnny Cash and Jerry Lee Lewis, to name a few."

Remembering how he felt to stand on the hallowed spot, Dominic adds: "To know that this is where it all happened, this is where the history of rock'n' roll was created. . .you can hear some of the recordings and they still sound as good today as when they were created.

"We then took a trip around Memphis. Ronny Light went with me and Gerry Crowley and his wife, Caroline. We didn't have a lot of time but we saw the area where Martin Luther King was assassinated. We went to the Rendezvous restaurant where Presley ordered his ribs and we visited the Peabody Hotel."

As well as being a museum for rock'n'roll the site of the Sun Records studio includes modern recording facilities where many major names have recorded. Would Dominic see himself recording there?

"I don't see myself recording at Sun. . .but then I didn't expect to be recording in Nashville. Now that I've been to Sun I think wouldn't that be nice? Who wouldn't?" ■

CHAPTER FOURTEEN

Where the Sidewalk Ends

THE story should have ended differently. The spring of 2001 should have found Dominic celebrating his arrival as a household name, thanks to the success of his first single to reach the UK Top 20. It's hard to find a sensible reason why it didn't happen.

Throughout the autumn of the previous year, Eamon Leahy was full of big plans for Dominic's second Nashville-produced album. There was going to be a new pop sound that would appeal to the Boyzone generation. There was going to be a £150,000 television advertising campaign. There was going to be a promotional tie-in with a leading chocolate manufacturer.

Most importantly, Dominic was going to release a single called *Buy Me A Rose* to coincide with Valentine's Day. Had just the last part of the plan been put into action, it's hard to see how it could have failed to yield a hit.

February is traditionally a good month for launching new careers in the music business. The reason is simple. Following the Christmas boom, CD sales are at a yearly low. With little cash to be grabbed, the major record companies avoid releasing product by their big name acts. However, there are still as many hours of radio airplay to be filled. There are still as many guest spots on TV and there are still as many slots on the charts. With few big name releases in the market place, there is less competition and, as a result, any new contenders stand a better chance of getting noticed.

A song specifically targeted at the Valentine's Day market would have an even greater chance of picking up airplay. And what could be a more fitting title for such a romantic occasion than *Buy Me A Rose?*

The song itself was a Grade A killer. Proof of its commercial power was that it had been a big American country hit the year before for Kenny Rogers. This was a particular achievement considering that 62-year-old Kenny was considered well past his sell-by date in a radio format that, for about a decade, had refused to play anybody over 40. Not only that, but Rogers didn't even have the backing of a major record company, having been forced to set up his own Dreamcatcher label just to get a release.

Despite its success across the Atlantic, Rogers' version of *Buy Me A Rose* had hardly been aired in Britain, and certainly not outside of the specialist country programmes, so the field was wide open for Dominic to make a run with what, to most listeners, would be a brand new song – and probably the most commercial song he had ever touched.

Being written in the modern Nashville style, *Buy Me A Rose* was not even overtly country – a term with a cowboy hat and cap-gun association that was still deeply pejorative in the minds of most UK radio people. It was simply a beautifully-crafted, warm-hearted, mature ballad about a man who works hard to give his wife material possessions only to discover that what she really needs is a little personal attention.

"What I look for in a song is something that every man would like to say to a woman and something that every woman would like a man to say to her," Kenny Rogers has said. And, on Valentine's Day, *Buy Me A Rose* would surely have done the talking for millions.

Even if mainstream radio had displayed its usual indifference to Dominic, the song should still have been a hit. As O'Donnell had done before him, Dominic had spent ten long, hard years building up a personal following on a massive scale. His tours pulled more fans to more venues across the UK than many well-known names with a dozen hits. And if 40,000 people were prepared to put their name to a petition to get Dominic on television, there were surely enough fans to buy his single in the week of release to ensure that it entered the Top 20 at a quiet time of year.

Once Dominic was on the chart, of course, the radio stations would have been forced to play *Buy Me A Rose*, and to their probable surprise they might have discovered that a lot of their listeners liked it. Dominic's sudden breakthrough after so many years of obscurity would then have made him newsworthy enough for national newspaper coverage and, probably, celebrity spots on prime time TV.

The strength of his fans' purchasing power was proven by the fact his album, *Stone In Love With You* entered the UK country chart at Number Six and quickly rose to Number Three. This was without the TV advertising campaign or chocolate box promotion that Eamon Leahy had planned and which, conspicuously, failed to materialise. That it didn't sell in even greater quantities in a much shorter period can only be attributed to the fact that many of Dominic's followers didn't even know the album was out until they turned up to see him in concert.

So, why wasn't *Buy Me A Rose* a hit? The simple answer is that it was never released as a single.

In April, Ritz belatedly deigned to press a two-track CD of *Stone In Love With You* and *Buy Me A Rose* for Dominic to take with him on promotional visits to local radio stations, but which was not available for public purchase. But by then, of course, the moment had long passed.

The question of why *Buy Me A Rose* was never released is harder to answer.

Dominic, himself, has seen too many unfulfilled plans and promises to do more than shake his head, shrug, sigh and open his hands in a gesture that says he has no answers. He must have been bitterly disappointed by the way in which his second Nashville album, *Stone In Love With You*, slunk on to the market without fanfare.

The only adverts for the album to appear in the country music press were tagged on to adverts for Dominic's tour dates. Since Ritz no longer booked Dominic's tours, even those adverts were paid for not by Ritz but by Stewart Laurie's Pinetree Promotions and Dominic's own company Demac Promotions Ltd.

Perhaps the most damning sign of how little effort was put into the launch of *Stone In Love With You* was that the UK's biggest selling country magazine, *Country Music People*, which in recent times had been a massive supporter of Dominic's music, was not even sent a review copy. Dominic was put in the humiliating position of learning this by chance and it was only due to his personal intervention that a review copy was eventually sent.

Talking generally of the market Ritz now operates in, Clerkin says, "It's a tough game, and it's tough at our end. You have to graft and graft away, and any opportunities that come along you make the best of them. Recording expenses are becoming much greater, as are promotional expenses and everything else.

"Going on television now is unbelievable," Clerkin continues. "And television is so fragmented with Sky and satellite television, you're never quite sure what people are looking at. If you want to go into something that you're guaranteed will get viewers, a 20-second ad in Coronation Street is something like 20 grand. And that's only in one region. If you want to go nationally, you're talking about a quarter of a million pounds for a 30 second ad – and if you blink, you miss it."

That explains why *Stone In Love With You* never got its TV advertising campaign. But it wasn't only television that had become fragmented in the 21st century.

Eamon Leahy attributes the record company's decision not to release *Buy Me A Rose* to their failure to get Radio 2 programmers to commit themselves to playing the single in preference to the Kenny Rogers version. However, he also thinks that the planned promotional push for *Stone In Love With You* fell victim to the upheavals that Ritz was going through as a company and which came to a head in December 2000 when Mick Clerkin sold his share in what had become the Ritz Music Group.

In a shrewd financial move Clerkin retained control of his core country 'n' Irish artists including O'Donnell and Kirwan, who would continue to record for Clerkin's Dublin-based Ritz Ireland with their product subsequently licensed to the London based Ritz Music Group for release in the UK.

The problems arose not just from a lack of effective communication between what were now two distinctly separate companies, but because RMG had diversified into many other areas. As well as running London's first 24-hour country radio station, the group also handled the UK distribution of a wide range of cult and mainstream American country music, from Emmylou Harris to Lonestar, through its acquisition of the Grapevine label and link-up with BMG. British middle of the road and pop performers such as Joe Longthorn and David Essex were also on the label and even rap music was part of the RMG output, with the result that even the hugely successful O'Donnell was now only one piece in a much bigger jigsaw puzzle. Country 'n' Irish was no longer the group's prime interest, and it was easy for a smaller player, like Dominic, to be overlooked.

The shame is that *Stone In Love With You* was a fine album and one into which the singer says he had more input in terms of the material than most of his releases. Foremost in his mind was the fact that the enormously popular Irish act, Boyzone, whom nobody would call remotely country, had cut a song called *I Love The Way You Love Me* by Nashville songwriter Victoria Shaw, and that the same band's lead singer, Ronan Keating, had enjoyed solo success with the touching ballad *When You Say Nothing At All,* which had first been cut by bluegrass singer Alison Krauss.

"I was listening to the charts," says Dominic. "I was picking up on Ronan Keating and the boy bands and what they were doing, and I was thinking, these are songs we all know. OK, they've got big machines behind them and they've got the opportunities to have them performed. But when you hear songs being recorded like *In This Life*, which you know Colin Raye has done, you think there has to be an audience for this.

"My attitude was, I can do this. I might not get the profile these guys are gonna get, but I can do these songs. I know I can do them well and, by doing them, it might open the door for some of the younger generation to accept our music.

The 40-year-old singer says, "I'm not looking to be that young, trendy teenybopper, because that part of my life has gone. But I was looking for good songs and commercial value, so at least a younger generation could listen and appreciate a good song.

"It is important for me to get songs that I can relate to. Because I'm a great believer in the words of a song."

Interestingly, five of the 16 songs on *Stone In Love With You* were co-written by Nashville writer, Skip Ewing, whose name had probably cropped up more often than any others in the credits of Dominic's previous albums.

"I think if I were a writer today, these are the songs I would write," says Dominic, who hoped to meet Ewing on his year

2000 visit to Nashville, but didn't. "I understood what he was writing about. "

Despite his fondness for the writer, however, Dominic confesses, that Skip's songs are difficult to perform. "Unless your ear is very strong you can lose a lot of time on it. I had difficulty with one or two of his songs."

By far the strongest Ewing co-write on the album, and every bit as commercial as *Buy Me A Rose*, was *Wish You Were Here*, another first-rate Nashville song that Dominic could have claimed as his own in the UK market place. The story was as simple as it was heart wrenching. In the first verse a man on a business trip buys his wife a postcard. On the front it just said *Heaven, with a picture of the ocean and the beach..* The chorus is the message of love he writes on the back. In the second verse, the man's plane crashes and a few days later his wife receives his postcard from Heaven. As a result, every line of the chorus suddenly takes on a haunting new meaning, right down to the tear jerking, *There's some folks we know, they say hello...*

Naturally, Dominic milked the sentiments without descending into the merely mawkish, in one of the most moving performances of his career.

While *Stone In Love With You* was ballad oriented, the album also included a couple of uptempo numbers designed to be incorporated into Dominic's stage show. Among them was a fresh and energetic cover of the Bellamy Brothers summer favourite, *Let Your Love Flow*.

The most innovative cover, however, was the John Hartford composition *Gentle On My Mind*. Among those who had enjoyed success with the much recorded classic were Glen Campbell, Eddy Arnold, Waylon Jennings, Tammy Wynette and Elvis Presley. But none had cut a version like Dominic's. In fact, even the musicians playing it didn't recognise it.

"That came down to the producer," reveals Dominic. "In the studio in Nashville they work on what they call the number system (as opposed to conventional musical notation). They get the name of the track and in some cases they listen to a form of recording so that they hear the melody. Once that's done they switch everything off and follow the number charts.

"But when it came to *Gentle On My Mind*, Ronny wouldn't let them listen to a track. He wouldn't let them hear it and he wouldn't let them know what the track was called. Because what you tend to do is go back to the first version that you heard. So, he had them get into a riff, the groove, on so many bars in one key and so many bars in the next key. Once they settled into that for about ten minutes of playing, he then let them know the song -and they basically fell off their seats! " said Dominic.

"What was really happening was the guys were creating the song themselves without knowing it, " continues Dominic, "I thought it was ingenious. I thought the technique was second to none. But I suppose that's a trick of the trade and that's what you pay producers for."

Another of Light's contributions to the album was the selection of the lilting and sentimental country song, *Ghost Of A Chance*, which proved an instant hit with Dominic's fans.

"I'd never heard that song before," says Dominic, "but the funny thing is, it's getting big, big requests at the moment, although I haven't performed it yet. When I listened to the song it wasn't as sophisticated as I had hoped, but when I heard the words I knew that certain regions would listen to it on radio. I knew it would be right for the album."

Far more modern in style and content, and perhaps the strongest song on *Stone In Love With You*, was *Don't Laugh At Me,* which Dominic had discovered at the Bluebird Cafe on his previous visit to Nashville. Dominic turned in a gripping reading of the highly emotive song which, like *Buy Me A Rose,* had every quality required for a potential smash hit.

With its heartfelt comments on school bullying and the plight of the homeless, the song would also be an ideal theme tune for a charity advertising campaign.

At the very least, *Don't Laugh At Me* deserves to be heard by a large audience. Sadly, it has yet to be released as a single.

It's a warm Tuesday in May, 2001. Wearing a loose open neck shirt, Dominic sits back on a park bench in Arleston Park, off the Old Mountfield Road in his home town of Omagh. As a local newspaper photographer crouches to take aim, Dominic rests his hand on the back of the new bench, just above the plaque that says it has been provided by The Samaritans as part of a new quiet seating area.

Explaining to a reporter his involvement in Samaritan Week, the singer remarks, "Through my work over the years and through the many letters I have received, I felt I could identify with the various reasons why people out there feel lonely and need someone to talk to. Samaritan Week is all about letting people know there is someone who is prepared to listen and I hope this venture will raise the awareness of the organisation locally.

For other pictures, Dominic crouches with council chairman Liam McQuaid to cut a ribbon leading to the new seating area, which has been funded by a grant from the National Lottery Board. He is also caught on film chatting unselfconsciously to a couple of local children and showing them how to tell the time with a dandelion clock.

Such scenes make it unsurprising that when a fan wrote to his fanclub newsletter asking which person, living or dead, he would most like to have met, Dominic didn't reply, Elvis, or another musical hero, but Princess Diana and Mother Theresa. He admires and also shares some of the human qualities that allowed them to relate effortlessly to the sick, poor, disabled and underprivileged without being patronising.

The opening of The Samaritans seating area in Omagh is just one of the many charitable works that Dominic undertakes, most of which go unreported and all of which he enters into without a thought of self promotion. Apart from the tens of thousands he raised for the victims of the Omagh bomb, Dominic has raised many thousands of pounds for other charities, large and small. In many cases, he has donated items of clothing, which have been raffled. In others, he has gone as far as standing in a supermarket and selling the famous Kirwan kisses at a pound a smooch (and 700 smackers in 90 minutes is a lip bruising achievement).

Wherever possible he tries to spend time with the organisers and beneficiaries of the charities involved, and in every instance he impresses with his genuine interest and sincerity.

Dominic has also touched the lives of many individuals. At home he has a set of folders containing letters from people who say he has helped them cope with illness, bereavement, disability or traumatic experiences in their lives through his CDs, concerts and the time he spends meeting his fans after his shows.

Never one to attempt to capitalise on the help he has given to others, Dominic doesn't say much about it. But those close to him say that the personal rewards he gets from helping people in such ways is a large part of what keeps him on the road so many days of the year.

At his home, before heading to Arleston Park, Dominic reflects on his career and the success he has seen in his first 40 years.

"I'm very pleased just to be here, and to have received everything that I have through the music industry. I would never have imagined that, starting off as a 16-year-old boy in a band, that I would have got this far.

"Where do you measure success? I see it as if it all stopped for me today, I have been successful. I have received much more than many other acts. I've toured with many international acts. I've performed in most of the major theatres. So, that has to be success in itself.

"Highlights?" Muses the singer. "I have so many great memories of working with all those acts that I've just spoken about. Just, basically, working in certain places. Walking on stage at the London Palladium. Working in the NEC with Kenny Rogers. The awards that I've picked up... Life really has been full over the years.

Looking ahead, Dominic says, "The future for me is still to be part of the business, to continue what I'm doing. I would like to try other things, be it radio or television. Even presenting. I think it would be nice to have that under your belt."

As for recording in Nashville, the singer says, "At the beginning, I thought, This is the first time and it will be a one-off album. And here I am, talking about going to do my third. I would definitely leave the book open on Nashville. "

On more personal matters, Dominic continues, "My plans for my children will always be to be there for them. To be around for them. I want to see them do well. I want to see them happy."

Predictably, they are all are interested in music, with second son Colm about to study at the prestigious Mountview drama school on the road to pursuing a career in stage musicals.

Although youngest son Jonathan is too young to contemplate what he'd like to do with his life, "Barry has got plans to be a drummer. He's talking about doing that through college as well. Lee, the oldest boy, loves music. He loves getting out on the road. He loves being part of the technical side of it. Maybe that's why he's studying computers at college. Maybe he will end up in the music industry, too."

Working with his dad, perhaps?

"I would hope not! "says Dominic with a laugh but admits it's very, very hard. I've been finding it hard for the last couple of years. It's been successful. It's done well. But it hasn't had the high spots in terms of chart success which I still strive for.

"Because of the way I have to work we have reached 182

shows a year... and it takes its toll, both mentally and physically. There are times when you feel very much burned up. And, to answer the question about Lee, I wouldn't want him coming into that lifestyle. OK, he would have to work, and that would be important, but I would like him to be able to look at it with a far more open mind about how and what you can do. If his early training has to be with me, and that's what he wants to do, then that's OK. But I'd like him to spread his wings."

For himself, Dominic can look forward to moving to his newly-built house on the outskirts of Omagh.

"I don't look at the material value of the house," says Dominic of the new property, which was almost complete. It's to make a home for the family. But, at the same time, it's another form of investment for years to come. If I was to end my career, I can look at it and think, well, look what I have. This is what I got out of it."

With that, we leave Dominic to set off for Alreston Park, to fulfil his duties on behalf of the Samaritans. After that, he's off to Belfast for four nights at the Opera House. Then it's on to a plane to record another album in Nashville and, perhaps, the breakthrough hit that he has searched for and deserved for so long.

Should the story have ended differently? For Dominic Kirwan the story is far from over. Upon his return from Nashville, he will hit the road once more. Stirling, Workington, Mablethorpe, Fareham, Worthing. There will be more theatres. More adoring fans. More autograph queues. More kisses. More sprigs of heather. More standing ovations.

Rest assured as you read this that probably tonight, at a theatre somewhere throughout the world, Dominic will be out there giving it his all. Singing his songs. Making people happy. Living the life that, as a teenager in Omagh, he once could only dream of. ■

For details of Dominic Kirwan's Fan Club
please write to:

The Secretary
D K Promotions
5 Bracken Close
Tamlaght
Omagh
County Tyrone BT78 5RR.

Acknowledgements

F IRST I must thank Dominic Kirwan for his time and frankness in the preparation of this book. In particular, I would like to thank him for not wanting to change anything except the spelling mistakes! I must also thank him for the many hours of enjoyment that he has given me through his concerts and recordings. It is the music that inspired this book and sustained me while writing it.

I would also like to thank the following people, witnesses to the tale, who gave generously of their time and memories: Philomena Begley, Terry Bradford, Barry Bradley, Theresa Brown nee Kirwan, Tony Byworth, Eamon Campbell, Mary Campbell nee Kirwan, Mick Clerkin, Alison Connor for putting even more miles on her car to bring me the files, Catherine DeLacy nee Kirwan, Keith Glass, Seamus Kerrigan, Elizabeth Kirwan, John Kirwan, Louise Kirwan, Stewart Laurie, Eamon Leahy, Pio McCann, Jim and Kath McLarnon, Jim McVeigh, Peter McGlone, Al Moir, Daniel O'Donnell, Declan O'Neill, Mike Perry, Rosaleen Pritchard (nee Kirwan) Jim and Lynette Rosie for the videos, Shaun 'Mudd' Wallace.

I must also thank the fans, who are so big a part of Dominic's story, and in particular those who shared their time, letters and photographs with me.

Finally, I must thank my editor and publisher John Jenkins for believing in this project from Day One. ∎

★ ★ ★

Photographs were generously supplied by Dominic Kirwan, Tony Byworth, and the Ritz Music Group.

We are the music makers.
We are the dreamers of dreams. . .
We are the movers and shakers
Of the world for ever, it seems.

Arthur O'Shaughnessy 1844-81: Ode (1874)